Fair or Foul the Weather

Brother Luke Slattery's Presidency of
St. Bonaventure's College, 1889 to 1895
The Diphtheria Epidemic, the Great Fire
and the Bank Crash

Brother J.B. Darcy

BOYS OF THE BLUE AND GOLD

Boys of the Blue and Gold,
Come join us in this chorus.
Here's to the days gone by,
Here's to the happy days before us.

Boys of the Blue and Gold,
let our motto be forever:
"Always pull together,
Fair or foul the weather,
Boys of the Blue and Gold,"

St. Bonaventure's School Song
by Brother J.C. Collins

Fair or Foul the Weather

Brother Luke Slattery's Presidency of
St. Bonaventure's College, 1889 to 1895
The Diphtheria Epidemic, the Great Fire,
and the Bank Crash

Brother J.B. Darcy

CREATIVE PUBLISHERS
St. John's, Newfoundland
1999

THE CANADA COUNCIL | LE CONSEIL DES ARTS
FOR THE ARTS | DU CANADA
SINCE 1957 | DEPUIS 1957

We acknowledge the support of *the Canada Council for the Arts*
for our publishing program.

Published by
CREATIVE BOOK PUBLISHING
a division of 10366 Newfoundland Limited
a Robinson-Blackmore Printing & Publishing associated company
P.O. Box 8660, St. John's, Newfoundland A1B 3T7

Printed in Canada by:
ROBINSON-BLACKMORE PRINTING & PUBLISHING

Canadian Cataloguing in Publication Data

Darcy, J.B., 1920–

    Fair or foul the weather

    Includes bibliographical references.
    ISBN 1-894294-13-0

1. Slattery, Luke.   2. St. Bonaventure's College (St. John's Nfld.)
— History.   3. College presidents — Newfoundland — St. John's
— Biography.   4. St. Bonaventure's College (St. John's, Nfld.) —
Presidents — Biography.
I. Title

LE3.S2485D37   1999   378.718   C99-950195-X

DEDICATION

To all those Priests, Christian Brothers, and lay teachers
who labored so diligently and successfully
to make St. Bonaventure's College
the magnificent institution
that it became,
and to all those
who are now engaged
in causing the College to rise
like a Phoenix
from its ashes.

Brother J.L. Slattery at the height of his powers

Table of Contents

Bishop T.J. Power, who asked the Christian Brothers to take over management of st. Bonaventure's

FOREWORD

*I*f a novelist, writing of a small city in a small country, were to cram into a seven-year period such calamities as a terrible epidemic, a devastating city-wide fire and the crash of all the country's banks, he would rightly be suspected of overstepping the bounds of dramatic possibility. Nevertheless, such were the traumatic events which formed the background for Luke Slattery's seven-year regime as President of the illustrious St. Bonaventure's College in St. John's, Newfoundland.

St. Bon's, as the College is familiarly known, was begun by Bishop Mullock in 1857 as a seminary-cum-academy for the Catholic boys of Newfoundland. Initially it prospered but by 1889 it was almost moribund, and in a last ditch effort to save it, Bishop Power asked the Christian Brothers to take over its administration, the Brothers having successfully directed St. Patrick's Hall Schools in the city since 1876.

Brother Luke Slattery, the principal teacher at the latter institute, was assigned the task of reviving the hallowed but dying institution. After taking up this responsibility, Brother Slattery wrote a constant stream of voluminous letters* to his Superiors in Ireland commenting on every facet of life in his adopted country. He possessed a most eloquent pen and poured out in these letters his hopes and fears, his successes and frustrations, as the disasters mentioned above inundated the College and defeated so many of his promising plans. So, while the focus of this account is on Brother Slattery and his work, it is in the context of what must be the most painful

---

* Copies of these letters are lodged in the Christian Brothers' Archives at Mt. St. Francis, St. John's. These letters, besides dealing with the internal affairs of the Brothers' communities and schools, are an invaluable source of information regarding the life of the country generally as seen by men who, while possessing great affection for the land of their adoption, were sufficiently detached from the local scene as to be able to give an objective assessment of the various situations and personalities involved.

period Newfoundland has ever undergone. To his gifted pen we are indebted for a graphic picture of the impact of these disasters on the life of the island and on individual citizens. Imbued with sympathy for the ordeals of the people, Brother Slattery's accounts are also unique. They relate events, not as historical, but as experienced by one who was personally undergoing the brunt of their violence and witnessing their impact on those around him.

Brother Slattery did more than just survive these disasters and make St. Bon's the premier educational institution of the island; even while faced with these challenges, he undertook broader initiatives which were to improve greatly the educational level of the entire country. His efforts and his warm-hearted generosity won the admiration of all who knew him, Catholic and Protestant alike, and made him arguably one of the most influential personages of his time on the Newfoundland scene.

It is Brother Slattery's letters which have formed the basis of the present volume and given it whatever value it possesses. I do not apologize, therefore, for quoting them at length where this seemed appropriate. I trust that this work will help present-day Newfoundlanders with their relatively comfortable standard of living to appreciate more deeply the tremendous trials which their grandparents had to overcome a century ago to make our present way of life possible. It is hoped also that it will enable the many graduates of St. Bonaventure's to realize more fully the debt they owe to those who made their alma mater the illustrious institution it became.

CHAPTER ONE

September – November 1889

"Not a room was furnished except by the spiders"

St. Bonaventure's College—known to one and all as "St. Bon's"— had already been in existence for thirty-two years when Brother John Luke Slattery arrived with two companions to take over its management in August 1889. When Bishop Mullock, O.F.M. had finished his magnificent Cathedral and "The Palace," his new residence next to it, he had opened the College on December 1, 1857 in the conveniently vacant "Old Palace" on Henry Street. This served as the College location while he prepared a permanent home for it in a new stone building on the Cathedral grounds, where the College was transferred on October 4, 1858.

As the College's first President, Bishop Mullock had surprisingly chosen a fellow Franciscan, an Italian whom he had known as a lecturer in St. Isodore's College in Rome. Father Enrico Carfagnini, or Father Henry as he was known to the students, knew little English, but had other admirable qualities which enabled him to get the College off to a successful start. After some years, Father Henry left the College, and a succession of fellow Franciscans and diocesan priests succeeded him, none of them particularly successfully, so that gradually the College began to lose its good name and consequently students as well. Ironically, its decline was hastened by the arrival of the Christian Brothers in St. John's in 1876. Their systematic teaching methods and professional approach at St. Patrick's Hall Schools attracted many students who would normally have attended the College. "How

1

is it possible," a prominent St. John's lady had asked Brother Slattery who was then teaching the senior class of about 100 boys at St. Patrick's Hall, "that you can do as much as three priests, two lay professors and a professor of drawing, and having more boys than they do?"

As the College building became more neglected and the debt ever heavier, the student population fell to an impractical level, and the attraction of capable staff became increasingly difficult. Bishop Power, who had succeeded Bishop Mullock in 1870, decided that he must either close the College or ask the Christian Brothers to take responsibility for it. For some of the local priests this was a traumatic decision, particularly for those who had attended the College in earlier, more halcyon days, so there was for a time fierce opposition to his proposal. But eventually wiser heads prevailed, the inevitability of the situation was realized, and the Brothers were officially invited to take over the management of the College in the spring of 1889.

The Brothers themselves were delighted at this compliment to their educational expertise, and great was their shock when their Superior General, Brother Maxwell, expressed serious misgivings about the project. They realized that their position in St. John's would be untenable if they did not accept the College after the Bishop had braved such opposition to offer it to them, and they eventually persuaded Brother Maxwell to agree reluctantly. Once having decided, however, he acted quickly and decisively. He appointed Brother Slattery as President and sent from Ireland to assist him Brothers Joseph Crehan and Andrew Prendergast, followed shortly by Brother Conrad Byrne, a "domestic" Brother to take care of the household arrangements. Brother Joseph was twenty-seven years of age at the time. An all-round genius, he was deeply interested in all branches of learning, one evidence of which is that he was probably the first person in North America to take an x-ray picture, the x-ray in question being that of Brother Andrew's hand, and the year 1896, Roentgen having discovered the x-ray in the previous year. Brother Prendergast was twenty years of age, a lively and effective teacher. Brother Byrne was forty-four. He began well but soon became more of a burden than a help to Brother Luke and his successors. He was the first Brother to die in Newfoundland and is buried in the Brothers' plot in Belvedere.

Brother Luke Slattery was, at the time of his appointment, a big, burly man of forty-two years of age, at the height of his powers. Born in 1847, he attended the Brothers' school in Nenagh, Ireland, and joined the Brothers at the age of seventeen. After his training and eleven years spent teaching in Dublin, he was transferred to Cork, and in his four years there he endeared himself to both Brothers and boys by his "good nature, happy disposition and thorough efficiency in the schools. He was kind, yet firm, agreeable and at times even jovial, never repellent, ever great-hearted and magnanimous."

He came to St. John's in 1881 to take over the senior class at St. Patrick's Hall Schools, where he taught with great success. In agreeing to become President of the College, he was well aware of the challenges he faced. He had been a close friend and confidant of Father Fitzgerald, who had been President of the College from 1881-1888 and had often spoken to him of his many difficulties. In writing the Superior General acknowledging his appointment, Brother Slattery voiced his concern:

> To regulate such an establishment, to bring the different elements of its necessary machinery into harmonious working, to raise an Institution like this from its present "abject condition" to one worthy of the Colony and of our Brotherhood, all these form a Programme far beyond my ability to accomplish. I clearly see the enormous difficulties before me.

But accept it he did, and events would show that Brother Maxwell had chosen wisely indeed.

On August 14, 1889, Brothers Crehan and Prendergast arrived in St. John's via the S.S. *Peruvian*. To acclimatize themselves, they moved briefly into Mount St. Francis, the

3

monastery for the Brothers teaching at St. Patrick's Hall. Then on August 29, Brothers Slattery and Crehan moved to the College to be joined two days later by Brother Prendergast. Their challenge began immediately:

> We entered here without a penny and had to furnish throughout as the priests took all their things away. We had not a book, nor a bed, for ourselves or the boys. Not a room was furnished except by the spiders.

Besides this, the building had been neglected in the disarray of recent times, so their first task was to get rid of the debris of years, and to clean and paint the various rooms, "tearing down and building up and making dingy places look bright."

On Sept. 9, the College was formally reopened by Bishop Power in the presence of many dignitaries including two of the original teachers from the 1850s, Father—now Archdeacon—Forrestall and Thomas Talbot, now High Sheriff. They must all have been delighted to find that there were fifty-five day-boys in attendance, a demonstration of the confidence the people had in the Brothers. Two weeks later, on Sept. 23, the boarders were admitted, the large dormitory on the third floor accommodating twenty-four and the small one on the same floor eight. On October 5, the "normals" arrived, bringing the total number of students to almost ninety. The "normals" were those older students preparing for the teaching profession, a preparation which up to that time had been haphazard enough.

Shortly after the opening, it was discovered that the cook had been acting dishonestly for years past. She was dismissed and Mrs. Leece, "an honest woman and a fair cook," replaced her. Mrs. Furlong was engaged as matron with Kate Power to assist her "and the College will never have better servants."

The situation of the normals was a peculiar one to modern ears. The ordinary boarders paid about forty dollars a year; the normals were supported by the government but at a lower rate. Some of them paid the difference themselves and

4

hence enjoyed all the privileges of the boarders, but the others slept in the attic (the fifth floor), ate at a separate table, polished their own boots and made their own beds. This traditional system endured for the first five or six years of the Brothers' regime when the distinction gradually disappeared though the normals continued to pay a lower "pension." The College Annalist relates an amusing incident in connection with the polishing of boots which indicates that schoolboy antics last from generation to generation.

> For the first few months a boy (hired) cleaned the boots, &, but as the boarders were utilizing him for bringing in contraband goods, he had to be dismissed and was replaced by Rachel Lynch who remained at her post in the College until the spring of 1902.

There was a related problem, Brother Luke reported:"Tobacco gave us a little trouble but I think we have completely eradicated old habits. But it requires continuous vigilance. The new comers give most trouble."

Together with the financial difficulties, and the frequent turnover of staff, the normals had always been one of the most serious continuing problems of the College. At times they had been housed in the College; at others they had been expected to board in the town.

> They were put out to board some few years ago and Dr. McDonald [*Bishop of Harbour Grace*] expostulated, saying that along with the dangers of such a system there was the positive loss of training and *polish* which residence in the College would supply. They were then made interns for a few years, but on Fr. Fitzgerald's departure were once more driven forth. Dr. McDonald has sent none since, (nor has Dr. Howley)[*Bishop of St. George's*].

Bishop Power and some of his priests, however, were opposed to permitting the normals to board. They considered them "low," "vulgar," "ill-conducted"; Brother Slattery did not agree. He believed that it was the system that was at fault and that "with judicious arrangements, and the supervision and training of the Brs. the habits and manners of the Normals would be as free from reproach as those of any other students." In a previous letter he had explained the source of the trouble, unintentionally revealing to what a sorry state the College had fallen under the previous regime:

> The "system" was wretched—each student supplied his own room—from bedstead to basin. The well-to-do folk made a flourish while the poor Normal should make his "appurtenances" correspond with the slenderness of his purse. Each was *supposed* to polish his own boots. Before entering—but for different reasons—neither class had often done this unenticing piece of work. The result was only what might be expected. Other matters, broken mugs and jugs, want of supervision in the dormitory and refectory, gave it a bad name & no wonder. Boys sick, at home, found all their bedding *absent* on their return. It was stolen and never recovered. Last winter a most respectable boy while out playing had his bedding stolen. He lay on the boards that night, got sick, went home and never returned. The untidy appearance of all things around was unjustly attributed to the Normals, but it was the System—or rather the want of any—that lay at the root. The soiled water left in the basins when the boys were going on last summer vacation, was there in the basins on their return, seven weeks later. Decent people turned against the whole place and its ways.

As it turned out, Brother Slattery was proved right, and before very long the normals were a credit to the institution.

Another decision of Brother Slattery's had an ironic twist. It will be remembered that for some years boys had been deserting St. Bon's in favour of St. Patrick's Hall. Now Brother Slattery decided to take in younger boys, both as day-students and as boarders, and the shoe was on the other foot. Boys began to leave St. Patrick's Hall for St. Bon's. Brother Fleming, the Superior of the former institution, was dismayed; he had lost both his principal teacher and his best students. He pleaded with the Superior General: "What will poor Mount St. Francis do if every man who can pay a pound is taken away. I fear our numbers will fall short....Our staff in St. Patrick's Hall will be very weak now—as soon as you can come to our aid."

To placate him, Brother Slattery agreed not to accept any boys not "in Fourth Book" and agreed that Brother Stanislaus Roche, the domestic Brother at Mount St. Francis, who had been transferred by the Superior General to the College over Brother Fleming's strenuous objections, should remain at the Mount.

Finances were also a worry. The Bishop had wanted the Brothers to accept responsibility for the entire debt but Brother Slattery objected, and it was agreed that the debt would remain with the Board while the College would pay the interest and gradually pay off the principal. The total debt amounted to $11,920, consisting of $9,556 in the building account and $2,364 in the current account. It was obvious that the necessary repairs, improvements, equipment, etc. would substantially increase this. But Brother Slattery was never one to dwell on financial problems; he trusted in Providence and the good will of the people. Among the improvements were "36 spring beds [iron] with wire and hair mattresses . . . eider down quilts . . . six new [closets] with an abundant supply of water . . . and another range of dry closets (four) so that if the frost beat us in the first we could abandon them for a while."

The boarders' daily regimen was worthy of any monastery: rising at 6:15 a.m., followed by morning prayers and a brief meditation on some passage of Scripture and a short period of study; then boots were put on and all trudged out to the Cathedral for Mass at 7:30, followed by breakfast at 8:00. School stretched from 9:10 until 12:30, followed by lunch, then school again from 1:00 to 3:00. Dinner at 3:15 was followed by recreation—usually cricket, handball or football—until 5:00 when house shoes were donned and there was study until tea at 7:00. This was followed by study again until 8:00 and indoor recreation till 8:30, a private reading period until 9:00, then night prayers—lasting about twenty minutes and consisting of rosary, litany, etc., and finally bedtime. Strict silence was observed from night prayers until after breakfast.

On Saturdays there was school or library from 10:00 a.m. until 11:00. On Sundays, Mass was at 9:00 and there was library from 10:30 until lunch at 11:30. At 12:15 there was a catechism lesson, and at 7 p.m. all attended Vespers in the Cathedral. From among the senior students a prefect was appointed whose principal duties were to lead the morning and night prayers and the walks on Saturday and Sunday afternoons.

Meals were hearty enough. Breakfast consisted of porridge and milk, bread, butter and tea; lunch of bread and butter and milk; dinner of fresh or salt meat, vegetables and either soup or pudding; supper of bread and butter and tea. The Brothers ate at one table, with the boarders at a second, and the normals at a third. There was reading from some pious or instructive book during breakfast and dinner. The bill of fare was excellent by the standards of the day; there was no more singing: "Old horse, old horse, what brings you here from Sable Island to Belvedere" as boarders had sung in previous years while residing at Belvedere monastery. The Brothers and the older boys carved the meat for their tables and served each other, with the matron taking care of the junior boys. According to Brother Slattery: "The *boys* liked it [the bill of fare] immensely. Indeed, *all* St. John's has given its approval. We may as well be living on the street side. I can't think anything has pleased the people more than the fact of our dining & with the boys."

On November 25, Brother Slattery was reporting to the Superior that "Everything goes on well with us here. One by one, our numbers growing steadily, so that we expect to record the full hundred after Xmas." It was just as well that he could not foretell the future for just a week later disaster struck.

CHAPTER TWO

December 1889 – July 1890

A Valley of Affliction

This city is now passing through a great trial. One can easily realize the times of plague, when the little white coffins two and three in the day, pass the door. You may see in the dusk of the evening a funeral with two persons following towards Belvedere. It is sad also to see the word "Diphtheria" in large letters on yellow posters stuck on every house affected. The magistrates have ordered this to warn people not to enter. It is a dreadful disease—whole families have been wiped out, not a child left to the distracted parents. No child under 14 yrs. is allowed to Mass or any such place, and much misery is caused by the dread of contagion.

*B*eing a seaport town with crowded housing and elementary sanitation, St. John's had frequently fallen victim over the years to epidemics of various kinds—typhoid, diphtheria, smallpox, scarlet fever, influenza and so forth. None of these, however, was more virulent than the diphtheria epidemic which raged during 1889 and 1890. And it is against this terrifying background that the next act in our educational drama was to be played out.

At first the epidemic attacked mainly the young; deaths were frequent. In April the Brothers in St. Patrick's Hall Schools reported: "The numbers in our junior schools are low. For the past three months diphtheria has been raging." By May: "Diphtheria spreading this week. Schools so thin we can't send returns.…Three men employed opening graves at Belvedere." A few days later: "They (the doctors) are sending a request this evening signed by all the medical men to have schools and churches closed for some time as Diphtheria is spreading so fast. … There is great consternation." By the 28, "This evening's account is, for the week, sixty nine new cases of Diphtheria and nine deaths.…All houses in which disease appears are to be quarantined, and children under fourteen not allowed to Churches." In early June, Brother Slattery reported that sixty-nine boys in St. Patrick's Hall Schools had caught the disease and nine had died. Later in the month he described two scenes he had just witnessed:

> Diphtheria is still raging. Yesterday a funeral passed—two little coffins side by side. Out of five children they were the third and fourth the poor parents lost. Today another sad sight. The funeral consisted of a man and two boys—the father and two *only* survivors of six children. It is most mysterious in its ravages and seems to be little understood by doctors. The people are panic stricken and fly all contact with the infected.

Some idea of the virulence of this attack may be gained from the fact that the usual number of deaths among those who contracted this disease was fifteen to twenty per thousand, while in this instance it was 180 per thousand. On July 3, a local newspaper reported that there had been 2000 cases of diphtheria (out of a population of 30,000), during the past twelve months, the number of deaths being 360 or about one for every day of the year. Between March 1888 and December 1889, according to the official reports, in St. John's and its environs: two families lost five members each; six families lost four members each; eighteen lost three each; fifty-two families lost two each; 235 families lost one each, while 679 families who were affected by the disease suffered no deaths.

During the summer of 1889, the children dispersed and the epidemic relaxed its hold, but as winter came on and the young gathered in schools again, it struck once more. Its impact on St. Bonaventure's College dramatically illustrates how the town as a whole must have suffered. On the last day of November, just as Brother Slattery and his companions were basking in the success of their initial efforts, the dread disease broke out among the boarders. School had to be cancelled, the day-boys sent home, the familiar yellow poster placed on the doors and all admittance refused except to priests and doctors. On December 8, Brother Slattery himself was smitten and the next day Brother Prendergast succumbed. Brother Slattery reported: "When we got it there were six boys down, and five of us lay down on one day—Andrew, myself, two servants, and a boy. So that eleven were down." Fortunately Brother Crehan remained immune through the attack and was able to assume responsibility for the care of the sick and other necessary details.

A week later, on the fourteenth, in an attempt to prevent the further spread of the disease, the seven still healthy boarders accompanied by Brothers Crehan and Byrne were evacuated to Friendly Hall, an isolated house located on Robinson's Hill outside the town. This move entailed a heavy expense since the Hall had to be equipped from scratch. Sadly, two days later, on December 16, one of the boarders remaining at the College died. He was George Gibbons, the son of a planter from St. Mary's, who had entered the College only three weeks previously. Altogether about seventeen boys and Brothers caught the disease. Fortunately, George was the only fatality, although another boy nearly died from erysipelas of the head brought on by the disease. The Matron had her own diagnosis of the cause of the outbreak. "The place was too clean," she told Brother Slattery, "If we were not so careful we might have been passed over."

Generally speaking the disease would work its way through its victim's system in the course of a week or two, depending on the severity of the attack, but its aftereffects could be as severe as the disease itself, could last much longer, and could take many shapes and forms. Brother Slattery described these effects in his letters home:

Diphtheria is as much to be dreaded for its consequences as for its immediate dangers. Curiously
enough these consequences may follow as heavily
from slight as from serious cases. With one boy, the
eyes are quite dim and he cannot read. Another is
quite powerless in the lower limbs. In my case, the
lungs were quite caught. Up to this time, conversation
for five minutes tires me out. Again and again, the
Doctor warned me that congestion of the lungs might
come on for the slightest cause. He would not hear of
my going to school.

And writing three months later:

Brother Andrew too is not so well. He was three weeks
out of school and even now is not looking well. The
diphtheria is still in his blood. Yesterday he got quite
weak on the walk and had to rest....
    Since then poor Andrew has not held his own. Four
or five days ago, he showed some feverish symptoms,
and has been in bed since Sunday. Today the Doctor
told me he had put a light fever over him.... As I write
he is much improved but it will take days yet, and
perhaps weeks before he is his old self. Just now the
most troublesome department is his hearing.

By December 22, the sick Brothers and boys were conva-
lescent enough to be moved, and they were transferred to
Friendly Hall, while the healthy group moved from there to
Silver Oak Lodge, a cottage near the College. Meanwhile the
College was thoroughly disinfected and Brother Slattery
hoped to be able to reopen for the New Year.
    But the enemy was not so easily defeated. Here is the story
in Brother Slattery's own words:

A boarder came from St. Pierre [Joseph Le Fèvre],
without previous notice, and as he had notes from the
priests and Brothers there, could speak no English

12

and knew no one in St. John's we were certain that there was no danger in admitting him. He was here over a week, and then complained. Not wishing to upset the house again, we sent him to hospital...poor Conrad [Brother Byrne] showed undoubted symptoms and the Doctor strongly urged to have him go to hospital...We agreed and have every reason to be pleased with the result. He is doing very well and most likely is over the worst....

I do not regret the case of the French lad—he tested the place and warned us of the danger lurking still. Had he not got it, we would now be in working order, and another outbreak with a crowded house might be far more fatal than the former. He was better in a few days and is now as well as ever. Thanks be to God! Forever! We had seventeen cases and one death, while the total in St. John's has been 2000 cases and over 400 deaths—one in five. Everyone ascribes that to the cleanliness and order of the place.

Seeing the hold this dreadful disease had got on the place, we looked around for some spot to rest our head—to resume our school work....So we have taken a cottage quite near by and are moving there this evening [*January 7*]. We will give a whole week to the fumigation and disinfection of this place, and hope to open the *day school* on Monday, January 20th. We will receive as boarders only those who have been sick and allow the others to board in town for a few weeks.

We owe an eternal debt of gratitude to the good people of St. John's—Catholic and Protestant, for the abundance of affectionate sympathy lavished on us during the past month.

So, my most dear Brother Superior, though we have passed through a deep valley of affliction and sorrow our hearts are not cast down and we look forward with confidence to bright days ahead.

In spite of his optimistic words, the effect of this calamity on Brother Slattery was shattering, especially the death of young George Gibbons. In a letter home, we hear him describe his feelings as well as his appreciation of the extraordinary devotion of the College doctor during the epidemic:

> Poor Dr. Shea has been a true friend—a brother—to us. One day when things looked bad enough, he and I were talking over each case. I am not ashamed to say that I was crying. He tried to cheer me up, but in the effort, completely broke down, and neither of us spoke for a long time. From early morning till midnight he was at our call.

Eventually when the disease had finally disappeared from the College, Brother Slattery reminisced:

> Even now my heart sinks when the sad remembrance of our fearful experience comes before me. I sometimes feel that I am only dreaming and that we are in reality still suffering the old trials. Now that we are free, I am not ashamed to acknowledge that I have often wept like a child when things seemed going from bad to worse. I cannot divest myself of the feeling that I am being punished for my inordinate anxiety last year to have the Superior accept the charge of the College. However, God is good and he has been very good to us. We might have a far sadder tale to record. Frs. Morris and Walsh—two splendid healthy young men lost their lives under similar circumstances, while at our daily roll-call no chair is vacant.

Still he found consolation in the tremendous support given the College by the people of St. John's:

> No one dare enter under fine of $50....But under cover of darkness, kind friends in numbers came to enquire and sympathise, and such loads of grapes and jellies, cases of wine and other necessaries, letters and

telegrams—all told the story of sincere sorrow.... As for the Catholics, well, our sorrow was theirs. In many a house special prayers and rosaries were said for us, along with Masses and Communions.

To make matters even worse the winter was "frightfully severe—far the worst within living memory." With it came the flu which struck down all except the indomitable Brother Joseph Crehan. Nevertheless, on January 20, the College reopened on schedule, only to have the furnace burst with the temperature at -13F, (-25° C). Still there was some compensation: "Again and again, he [*Dr. Shea*], told us take punch and spirits and we carried out his orders to the letter. But such quantities of port!! Even the youngest boy had to get four glasses a day!"

By the 17 of February, 1890, Brother Slattery could report to the Superior General that, "Thanks be to the good God, our clouds are fast clearing, and brightness and happiness resuming their old position."

Courageously, in spite of this turmoil and his own bouts of illness, Brother Slattery had seized the opportunity of the vacant weeks to alter radically the physical setup of the school. He wrote to Brother Holland on March 4:

The boys' entrance was away round at the back. It is now in front, opposite the avenue, a saving of about 100 yards, besides being at the shady side. The old kitchen & parlour make a lovely school and a most unsightly room is taken away. The large school room is divided into two and looks well. The windows at the end were closed to admit of a ball court outside. We have had them opened and they give splendid light and ventilation to what was a very dark and musty school room. Over the gymnasium is the Library. Over the kitchen are the servants' quarters—completely away from the main building, and having no communication whatever with it except across the ambulatory or play Hall. I look upon this as a most important arrangement.

These changes were a vast improvement and delighted all who saw them. Writing on April 1, Brother Slattery was cautiously optimistic. "I am very hopeful that we will have a hundred [students] after Easter, and that the old prosperous days will return to us." But he warns: "Diphtheria still rules. Yesterday a Protestant minister and two of his children went to the hospital. Three days before another child of his died."

When school did reopen on April 14 after the Easter recess, Brother Slattery gave an interesting picture of the day-to-day life of the College:

We reopened on yesterday and have much reason to be pleased. We had near eighty and all in good spirit. About two dozen are boarding, and with the Normals we will have over thirty in the house. We have been most fortunate in getting a splendid Matron. She, with another servant, looks after the cleanliness of the whole house, and I can sincerely assure you there is not a cleaner or neater house in the Society. We have two tables. The grown boys carve and look after one another, but the matron carves for and attends to the younger section. Then at the top of the room, on a raised platform, is the Brothers table—overlooking all. There are four women altogether so that every place is properly attended to. People are much taken with the complete change that has been made in the appearance and care of the College. I wish we could do something with the field in front. You know it is very uneven and hilly and unfit for cricket or any such game. Yet I am afraid to move as I cannot give time from the school and Conrad is a very—well—a very *holy* man. I am sure holiness is a most excellent quality, but a little *activity* tacked on would be a great blessing.

As can be seen from many of his letters, Brother Slattery was not happy with the apparent inactivity of Brother Byrne (which may well have been due to the aftereffects of diphtheria). At one point he commented ruefully: "His machinery never hurts anyone by its velocity."

Brother Slattery was already planning future improvements. But his caution was well justified. His old enemy still had a sting left in its tail. Brother Slattery's dramatic account of its last visitation and of the way he dealt with it could hardly be bettered:

> What then disturbs us? Only another case of our old visitor *diphtheria*!! One of the day boys was attacked but of course that did not upset us very much. But a few days after as I made my nightly round I noticed one of the Boarders who sat beside the former, a little flushed. He said he was not sick—only a little head ache, and on further pressing pleaded guilty to a slight soreness in his throat. He is a fine little fellow—one of those to brave out an attack never acknowledging a fall. All were in bed. I got hot water, bathed his feet & gave him a hot drink. Before this I had carried him—body and bones, blankets and all, down to a little room near my own. I slept little that night as from the appearance of his throat I feared the worst. Next morning—there stood all the symptoms of diphtheria—two big white patches on the tonsils.
>
> We had 87 in school the day before, and my heart sank as I realized what those marks meant. All scattered again, the awful yellow poster on the door—the isolation, quarantining &, &. Yet there were the marks, his temperature 102½, his pulse 120. To send him to hospital meant closing for 14 days at least, as the Board of Health should order. To keep him meant—I knew not what. We disinfect all parts of the College frequently so my first step was an abundant dose all over the house. Just look at me, in spirit, as I sit by the poor little fellow, reasoning out what was to be done. To send for the doctor meant official declaration of the disease. One course suggested itself—keep him quiet and tell no one.

The risk was great, but I would run it or destroy all prospect of success, a least for a long time. I know the pathology of diphtheria pretty well now, so I put myself and the boy in God's hands and kept the secret. I knew there was no fear of the boy so I determined not to get the Dr. till *danger* appeared. I disinfected the surroundings, the boy, myself—again and again, found excuses for isolation and nursed him day and night. With diphtheria, port wine is as molten lead, yet it is the best medicine. The brave little fellow took it like a hero, though I knew what it cost him. I had no trouble with him as to *taking* things, and after three days all was well! Three days more he was as well as ever and is in school today. Neither he nor anyone in the House knew what was the matter. All the time I had a school to mind, as Joseph can take only a class and Andrew is not strong. Today all goes well—had I got the Doctor, we would be closed perhaps till summer and the College would get the name of being unhealthy.

Well, I am nearly tired out—but thanks be to God for ever and ever. When I think on "what might have been," I feel very grateful to God. Had I not noticed him so soon, it would have got into his system before morning and the worst might come on....Will you say a prayer for this unfortunate College, so sadly darkened by the clouds of sickness lying around us.

An enormous risk to take but it seems to have come off. His enemy had finally acknowledged defeat and retired to lick its wounds. So for a short while—a very short while, he and the College were at peace.

On June 10, however, came another bolt from the blue. Brother Slattery received a letter from the Superior General which would, in more normal times, have been a source of gratification, but in the present situation filled him with dismay. Every ten years, elected representatives of the Brothers around the world were summoned to meet with the

Superiors to discuss the state of the Congregation and to formulate plans for the future. This meeting was, and still is, called a General Chapter. The letter informed Brother Slattery that he had been elected to this Chapter and that he was to leave for Ireland as soon as possible. Brother Slattery responded:

> When I looked round and saw all the details which require attention during the coming vacation, the feeling of dismay took the place of all others. This I hope is the last accident or obstacle raised up against our success here. The sickness was bad enough, but to go away and leave the place, so unsettled, with only the new hands to look round and meet priests and people of whom they know little is really a *misfortune* not to be despised.

He lamented: "Surely, there were 'wise men (enough)in Israel' without calling on the undersigned." But he bowed to the inevitable and on the 25th of the month set sail for Ireland. Doubtless the sea voyage with its enforced leisure did more to restore his health and spirits and to prepare him for the coming year than any of his own plans could have done. So ended his most remarkable and calamitous first year as President of the College.

The first Christian Brothers staff of St. Bonaventure's; L-R: Brother J.L. Slattery, Brother P.J. Culhane, Brother T.A. Pendergast, Brother J.J. Crehan

CHAPTER THREE

September 1890 – July 1891

Reinforcements arrive – the enemy strikes again

*B*rother Slattery returned from Ireland refreshed by his long sea voyages and by his visit to his homeland and friends. During his absence two Brothers had been added to his staff, Brothers Baptist Flood and Joseph Culhane. Brother Flood had been teaching the second class in St. Patrick's Hall since his arrival in St. John's in 1881. During all that time he had suffered much from ill health due to the threat of tuberculosis (TB), and in the spring of 1890, on the doctor's recommendation, the Superior had decided to recall him to Ireland, much to Brother Flood's regret. He was very fond of Newfoundland and its people. However Brother Slattery had other ideas and wrote to Brother Holland:

> Poor Brother Baptist is not at all well. I suppose you know what the Doctor recommends. If the Supr. would not think it impertinent on my part, I would ask to give Baptist a trial for a while at the College. He would be of service about music and singing till you could send one able for work. It would be easy for him, and we would take every care of him.

Bishop Power reinforced Brother Slattery's suggestion and the Superior agreed to the transfer.

The other new member, Brother Patrick Joseph Culhane, was born in Glinn, County Limerick in 1868, and had entered All Hallows seminary in Dublin in 1887. Not finding the peace of mind he had anticipated in the clerical vocation, he transferred to the Christian Brothers in September 1889, and at the end of his novitiate year was sent to join the College staff. At the time he was a very inexperienced twenty-two-year-old but, as time would prove, another excellent choice for the College and one who was to have a profound effect on its fortunes in later years.

Brother Slattery was delighted. At the end of September he could report: "Our classes are in excellent working order. We can reach all our work now." By the end of November there were ninety-seven students on the roll, including forty boarders. The traditional Distribution of Prizes, which had been postponed from the previous July because of Brother Slattery's enforced absence, took place just before Christmas. Traditionally, part of this event was an elaborate concert and the Bishop, with his usual caution, decided that it should be held in private with just himself, some priests and members of the College Board present. He wanted to test for himself whether, under the new administration, it was worthy to be presented to the public. Fortunately it passed off very successfully, and in the following years the Bishop would want it to be as public as possible.

At about the same time the School Inspector, Mr. James J. Wickham, examined the College, and his report was highly laudatory, giving a detailed overview of the work of the College under the new regime. Read today, it provides as well an interesting comparison between the course of studies of one hundred years ago and of the present. The report is given in full in Appendix A.

After noting that expenditure exceeded income by almost $1000, the report pointed out that this $1000 had been spent on purchasing scientific equipment. It would appear that the Brothers' well understood the importance of scientific studies.

The field in front of the College had been levelled (in spite of Brother Byrne), and the "Bishop's garden," which was situated where the Forum and its parking lot now stand, integrated into the school property. Bishop Power had donated this garden, thus rounding off nicely the College grounds.

Attendance had risen to 116 including twenty-seven boarders and twelve student teachers. Drawing was taught in all classes. In singing classes, the newly developed Tonic-Sol-Fah system had been introduced for the first time in Newfoundland by Brother Flood. The students were grouped into five classes; the highest, with only six pupils, was preparing for the London Matriculation Examinations, something which had not been attempted in Newfoundland in recent years. The Inspector had examined all classes over a period of four days and expressed his "unqualified satisfaction" with the standard of achievement he had witnessed.

He was equally high in his praise of the College's approach to discipline which, he reported, "is equally removed from that undue stringency and espionage which generally breed distrust and antagonism and that mistaken laxity so conducive to the growth of careless or vicious habits."

But while the College was still basking in this praise, the old enemy struck again. In February two of the boys showed symptoms of diphtheria. They were light cases and Brother Slattery followed his previous practice of isolating them in the sick bay and caring for them himself. Again his tactics worked and within a week the boys were well. In March he had a more serious scare. Diphtheria was once more prevalent in the town; there were sixteen children down with it in Belvedere girls' orphanage, and Brother Slattery was keeping an anxious eye on the boys. "I am afraid," he wrote, "if I saw the yellow notice on our door that my heart *would* break. It means *so* much!!!"

But take every precaution that he could, the College was not to escape. At the end of April he had to admit to the Superior General:

> I know you will be very sorry to hear that our old enemy diphtheria has taken a fall out of us at last. Going my rounds last Saturday night, I noticed one of the boys. On questioning him he pleaded "not guilty to any form of sickness." I told him remain in bed the

following morning till I came to him. Next day he still persisted in being all right and against my will he came down to breakfast. I knew there was something wrong and kept my eye on him. At last, about noon, he had a headache and was sick. He was put to bed and towards evg. the *sore throat* came on. I saw at once his case was serious and got the Doctor. Yet, *he* could not pronounce till Monday morning. Well he had the sickness certain and was at once removed home. We dismissed the Day Boys and here we are in quarantine. The Yellow poster on the Hall Door, no one may enter or leave unless the priest or doctor. No leper of olden time was so cut off as we are now. But, only for a few days. If no further case occurs we will get a clean bill of health this week and resume work next Monday. So far (Thursday) no sign of any other case, so I hope we will lose only the one week. Of course the Boarders & Normals are at work. The boy is a nephew of Dr. Howley's and was not strong. Hence my fears for him. but thank God, he is all right. The Doctor said that the prompt measures taken, hot baths, drink, perspiration & took the sting out of the attack and most likely saved the boy's life. Our good Bishop and all the priests came one after another to sympathise with us, but today it is all congratulation at our escape. When I tell you that there were seventeen new cases in town last week and *four deaths* you will understand how fatal are its attacks. Twenty five per cent is a heavy mortality.

I send you the Inspector's Report for last year. You will be pleased with the accounts of the College. The Inspector has been very friendly to us all along and is enthusiastic in his admiration of the Bros' work. If this frightful scourge diphtheria only stayed its persisten, attacks we would have a clear field, but as it is, and has been, it is a continual fight. Nothing but the most unceasing care and watchfulness has preserved us but God has been very good to us—things might have been far worse. *One case* has put us to great trouble—but I have put nearly a dozen through my hands unknown to any one. I need not tell you that before assuming such responsibility I see my way clearly to a successful termination. At the least sign of danger the doctor would be called. Under God, I attribute this wonderful safety of the sick boys to the continual watchfulness and prompt action taken.

Two months later Brother Slattery was happy to report that, "Diphtheria has almost disappeared as there were only four cases in the City during last week—no deaths. But it will come round again when least expected. Several deaths from La Grippe [*A name commonly given to influenza*]." His experience had taught him caution.

With such difficulties and with so much else to attend to, one would not expect Brother Slattery to have time or energy to take on other projects. On the contrary, during the same year he took on two major initiatives, one more or less forced upon him, and the other a project of long standing.

Scholarship Group 1896
Standing: Ronald Kennedy, Michael Connolly
Seated: George Kearney, William Kitchin, John Fenelon

CHAPTER FOUR

September 1890 – July 1891

Looking towards the future

*I*s there something about the end of a century which inspires communities to cast a jaundiced eye on their most cherished institutions and to be tempted to jettison them in favour of those of other communities? This has happened in Newfoundland in education matters throughout the 1990s, the rationale being that the youth of the province must be better prepared for the twenty-first century. What is perhaps not so well known is that exactly the same scrutiny took place at the end of the nineteenth century, with the same groupings involved and the same arguments presented from either side. Then as now, powerful forces in the country combined to urge the adoption of a unified public school system instead of the denominational system. As Brother Slattery described the crisis of the 1890s: "There is a strong party here trying to secularize the schools and to destroy their denominational character. Unfortunately many schools—indeed all—offer sufficient grounds for the proposal," And again in a description weirdly prophetic of the events of one hundred years later: "The Wesleyans are strong, progressive and aggressive here, and pushed on this question hoping to introduce the system established in Nova Scotia and the other Maritime provinces...Some of their lay members in the House of Assembly have made a noise too about the defects of the present system." The difference between the two centuries is that, in 1891, instead of imposing a new system on the people, the government of the time prudently sought the advice of the

27

people and offered prizes for the best essay containing "Suggestions as to the Improvement of Education in Newfoundland."

Recognizing the importance of this issue, Brother Slattery urged the Bishop and the priests to respond but none were prepared to do so. He then decided to take up the challenge himself in order to preserve the traditional denominational system and show how it could be a success. After drafting his ideas and discussing them with the Brothers, Brother Slattery showed them to the Bishop who gave his enthusiastic approval and then submitted the proposal to the government. Brother Slattery's essay begins with perceptive reasons for maintaining the denominational system, and a word of warning to which our legislatures in the 1990s might with benefit have taken heed:

> There is a system of Education established in the Colony which, on the whole has done good work. If the results are not satisfactory, the cause may be found in the apathy of the people, and in the circumstances of the Island. With all its defects it may be claimed for this system, that it has not caused any ill feeling among the members of the different religious denominations, and that no charge of proselytism under its wings has been made.
>
> Many persons advocate the abolition of the denominational principles on which it is based. They forget the cost of the risk. Each religious body has made great and praiseworthy efforts, and has expended vast sums of money in furtherance of its particular views regarding Education. Without noticing the work of former times, witness the splendid new college raised by the Methodists, St. Patrick's Hall and the schools in Riverhead by the Catholics; and the fine building erected near the Synod Hall by the members of the Church of England. Looking through the Island, the educational establishments, not erected on the denominational principle, are

conspicuous by their absence. Uproot this principle and private efforts are at an end. This is the one green spot in the great desert of dependence on government for supplying every want, public and private....

Any material change in this matter will disarrange the present machinery, create distrust, and perhaps stir up religious discord. If we look to some of the neighbouring provinces, notably Manitoba and Ontario, not to mention the United States and some countries of the Old World, the frightful risk will be seen of having an education system out of harmony with the feelings of any considerable section of the population.

He then proposed his ideas for improvement, ideas which are models of moderation. Some of them might well have been applied to solving the educational dilemma of the 1990s in a manner reasonably acceptable to all involved.

For the first time in Newfoundland, teaching was to become a profession rather than a "job." Teachers were to be adequately paid according to their qualifications, and after thirty years service were to receive a suitable pension. Scholarships were to be given to encourage young talented people to take up the profession.

In general, inspection was to be done by district rather than by denomination. Foreshadowing much later developments, Brother Slattery suggested that in areas where no one denomination could support a school, there should be common schools with a mixed Board. Common competitive examinations were to be established, and a central Board set up to certify teachers, oversee examinations, oversee the opening of new schools and supervise the distribution of government grants. He offered some shrewd advice: "On no account should it be connected with the Government. Should it be so connected, politics would glide in imperceptibly and party spirit rule in a matter that should be above party and the heart of politics." (The full document may be seen in Appendix 2.)

Brother Slattery's paper was accepted as being the best submitted, and the government prepared a bill based on it, though Brother Slattery with his customary keen insight declared: "the Government are going to introduce a bill entirely on the lines of the Essay. But I am not so sure of their sincerity in trying to pass it." Nevertheless the government did do so, though with many alterations and emendations, and so it came about that the Newfoundland educational system in vogue for the past hundred years has been fundamentally based on Brother Slattery's ideas. He deserves great credit for laying the basis for transforming the practice of teaching in the Colony into a true profession. It was just at this time that the present Newfoundland and Labrador Teachers' Association was being formed, and Luke was invited to address their first convention. As he wrote:

> The Wesleyan teachers will hold a convention in July. Some Protestant [i.e., Anglican] & Catholic teachers, to promote their common success, have allied themselves with them and formed a teachers Association. They have invited me to give them a lecture at their coming convention...I must pull it off as best I can.

Evidently they appreciated his efforts on their behalf.

Brother Slattery's second important initiative during this period involved a separate but related issue. He realized only too well that, with the newly awakened interest throughout the world in providing education for the ordinary citizen, the struggle to obtain a continuing supply of Brothers from Ireland was likely to be a long and difficult one. Newfoundland was in competition with Bishops from every part of the English-speaking world who were besieging the Brothers' superiors in Ireland with requests to open or take over schools for their Catholic children. On the other hand, he had been pleasantly surprised, when taking over the administration of the College, to discover that the students were very amenable and unusually pious: "Many of the boys are very pious and good. All go to Holy Communion monthly and most of them have an appointed time for a visit to the Blessed Sacrament. There are seven or eight at present who are studying with a view to the priesthood." And: "Above all the 43 who board with us, I must praise as the best boys I ever met. Some of them have their little faults but on the whole they are excellent." He gave a practical example:

> When we were going on Retreat two boys asked to go with us "to the desert" and we consented—but only for 3 days [The Brothers made a seven-day retreat yearly]. One by one others joined on till we had twenty three!! Many of these have ideas for the priesthood and others for ourselves. Well, I was never more edified. Many of them scarcely left the Chapel, till out of mercy, they were sent to walk round the grounds. As for Rosaries, Stations, &, it was one exercise from morning till night. One great blessing we have is that all our *grown* boys are either for the priesthood or religion and are most edifying. The younger ones easily follow.

The presence of this suitable material, added to the difficulty in getting enough reinforcements from Ireland, had persuaded the Brothers that they should attempt their own house of formation for candidates for the Congregation. It will be appreciated that this was a more complicated venture than simply the provision of teacher training courses for those interested in becoming Brothers. Though such courses were, of course, essential, it was even more necessary to create an environment where the young men could grow in faith and morals and develop a deep spirituality according to the particular approach of the Congregation. For several years the Brothers had been pressing this matter on the Superior, and in November of 1890 Brother Slattery wrote the Superior General asking permission for the venture and outlining plans for implementing it. A start could be made with a group at St. Bon's under the direction of Brother Crehan. He pointed out that since the young men would be student teachers, it would be possible to get the government to pay for their keep, and they could do their teacher training at St. Patrick's Hall Schools.

Eventually the Superior agreed and on the 25 of May 1891 Brother Slattery could write the Superior: "Well, thank God, we have moved a little about the postulants. There are four put apart, on the lines I suggested to you....They are all excellent boys whom we have known for years. So far everything has gone well with them."

Bishop Power had given every encouragement but prudently had suggested that they wait until after the vacation before asking Rome for definite approval to set up a novitiate. The idea proved successful and all through Brother Slattery's regime there were rarely less that four or five candidates in residence.

The arrangement lasted, with various ups and downs, until Brother Slattery's successor, finding it too much of a burden, suppressed it. Though all those who applied did not persevere, it provided several excellent Brothers who gave long service not only in Newfoundland but in various parts of the world. One cannot but wonder what impact this system might have had on the educational development of Newfoundland and elsewhere if others in authority had had Brother Slattery's appreciation of its possibilities and given it more enthusiastic support.

In spite of all trials and tribulations, 1891 continued on a very upbeat note, with an improved educational system owing much to Brother Slattery's inspiration, and with commencement made on a local recruitment program for the Brothers. The climax came on St. Bonaventure's Day, July 14, when the Brothers held their first public Distribution of Prizes, though even this was not without its disappointment. Bishop Power was at odds with Governor O'Brien and objected to his being invited, leaving the Governor, who was a good friend and admirer of Brother Slattery, wondering, in Brother Slattery's words, "what he had done to offend me." Still, he reported that the distribution was:

an *unqualified success*...Our good Bishop is delighted and never stops expressing his pleasure...I do not exaggerate when I say that *all* St. John's were delighted with our first public Exhibition. The Bishop, Rt. Rev. Mon. Howley, and about twenty priests were present. All these as well as the members of the College Board were afterwards at Dinner.

All of this gives some idea of the pressure there must have been on Brother Slattery to succeed, and his relief when it came off so well.

And indeed he needed this encouragement for, in spite of his previous experience with disasters, the catastrophe that loomed on the horizon surpassed anything he could ever have imagined.

Ruins of St. Patrick's Hall after the 1892 fire

CHAPTER FIVE

September, 1891 – July, 1892

Tried in the Fire

Exactly forty-six years and one month had passed away since the great fire of 1846, and the inhabitants of St. John's had come to look upon the fire demon as one that would never again destroy any great portion of our city. We felt secure in the great water power we had, and the almost unlimited quantity which was stored in the natural reservoir at Windsor Lake (Evening Herald, Sept. 10, 1892, quoted in D.W. Prowse, *A History of Newfoundland*, 1895, p.523).

*T*he 1891-2 school year began peacefully enough with no indication of what lay in wait at its close. There were the usual minor difficulties. Brother Conrad Byrne became ill and Dr. Shea recommended that he return to Ireland. In unconscious irony the Doctor stated: "Another winter will go hard with one like him who takes so little exercise." But Brother Byrne stayed in Newfoundland and did not die until twenty years later—so much for the infallibility of doctors. In July 1891, the College had taken the plunge and entered four boys for the London University Matriculation Examination. These exams were no ordinary tests. A writer in *The Evening Telegram* two years later (July 17, 1893) commented: "Till a few years ago, these examinations were allowed to pass unnoticed, and when six students, four from St. Bonaventure's and two from the Church of England

College, went up, people shook their heads and laughed at them for so doing."

In this first effort none of six candidates passed, but the results were very encouraging for the College since its candidates had come so "near the mark" and had beaten the candidates from both the Church of England and Wesleyan Colleges. Brother Slattery claimed: "I have no doubt that next year one of ours will take the Exhibition (£200 stg). All ours are going on again."

In his report of the affairs of the College to the Superior on Christmas Eve, one can almost feel the joy and astonishment Brother Slattery felt at the change that had taken place since the Brothers took over the management of the College:

> When I reflect on our beginnings here and on our awful state of sickness and abandonment just two years ago, I am simply astonished at [the] wonderful change we now experience. Since then everything has gone well with us. Never, since its foundation was this College so high in public esteem and confidence. From our beloved Bishop and his priests to the humblest of his flock, we have only friends and affectionate well wishers. We have now 115 boys and find ourselves much pressed for accommodation in Schools and House. What is best of all, our boys are good and edifying in their conduct and behaviour. Above all, the 43 who board with us, I must praise as the best boys I ever met. Some of them have their little faults but on the whole they are excellent.
>
> We have sixteen pupil Teachers who I hope will make good, efficient instructors in the various districts to which they will be ordered. The four little postulants are as good as gold.

Moreover, Brother Slattery had been able to re-establish good relations with the Governor by asking him to act as patron of a concert that was being put on to reduce the College debt.

The year drew triumphantly to its close with the consecration of Dr. Michael Howley as Bishop of Amastria and Vicar Apostolic of St. George's. This was the first time a native Newfoundlander had been raised to the episcopacy and there was tremendous rejoicing throughout the island. The College had a particular reason to share in the rejoicing. Bishop Howley was the first ex-pupil of the College to be raised to that dignity, having been a pupil when the College first opened its doors in the "Old Palace" in 1857.

On June 28, the new Bishop was welcomed by the students with a gala concert. The students performing included such future well-known figures as Fred Jardine, Andrew Jordan and George Bradshaw. The orchestra consisted of four violins, four pianos, two cornets and one clarinet.

Then on July 8, just as the school was preparing to close down for the summer, disaster struck not just the College but the entire city. The College annalist notes the event with astonishing brevity. His entry for that date reads: "At 4 p.m. a fire broke out and burned half the city." But Brother Slattery, in reporting the event to the Superior in Ireland, painted a vivid picture of the scene, one which could have been taken from Dante's *Inferno*:

St. John's is wiped out—except about ¼ of the worst part. A man lighting his pipe in a hay loft began it, then a strong wind did the rest. Weeks of burning weather had prepared the blaze—10,000 people are homeless, thousands of respectable people are paupers. The Protestants have lost their grand Cathedral—the pride of the city—their schools, halls, &. The Wesleyans are wiped out, also the Presbyterians. The Catholics were shielded by the arms of God—our noble Cathedral, convents, schools, College, the Mount, all are safe. But dear St. Patrick's Hall with all its loving memories and proud associations is no more. Its walls stand and with £8000 insurance will soon rise from its ruins. For three hours we fought to save it. The apathy of the people, or rather their hopeless despair was frightful. But the Bros. fought like heroes. Again and again, we put out the burning spots, till the houses to windward set it on fire under us. Out from the grand Hall we came, black as Negroes, drenched & fainting. A moment more & retreat was cut off—as it was the smoke suffocated us.

Brother Slattery was reticent about his own part in the fight to save St. Patrick's Hall, but one of his companions writing in the *Christian Brothers Educational Record* in 1927 described in graphic detail the fire and Brother Slattery's heroism in the attempt to save the Hall. He noted also the part that the College boarders played in the effort:

For weeks the weather had been very warm; there was not a drop of rain; immense areas of the inflammable spruce and var (the turpentine spruce) were on fire inland. A hot wind blew steadily seawards. A few minutes after five one evening a shed on the plateau above the town took fire. In a few minutes the flying sparks ignited the roofs of several houses along the edge of the plateau; from these, again, the sparks, carried by the wind, dropped here and there on the tarred house-tops. In an hour or two the flames raged in the path of the breeze and spread to right and left From the top of the tower of St. Patrick's Hall towards the Narrows nought was seen but a vast extent of flames and smoke and flying brands, a veritable inferno. The fire brigade was helpless. The Brothers manned the roof of the Hall; the College boarders formed a line, and buckets were passed from hand to hand to the roof. A spurt of flame flickered in one of the corners of the wooden moulding on the top of the tower. This required instant attention. An iron railing enclosed the top. It was intensely hot. Wet blankets were thrown across it. They acted as a protection from the heat and glare of the flames raging across the street, far to right and left, and down to the water's edge.

Over the railing and on to the curving top of the dormer windows, jutting out from the little curving mansard roof of the tower, Br. Luke climbed. He stood sixty or seventy feet above the ground on his small arching support not more than a foot wide. Time after time, balancing himself on this precarious ledge, he flung a bucket of water up at the blazing corner. Just as the fire was vanquished at this point, eddying wreaths of smoke were whirled up the stairs, and the alarm was raised that somehow the joists of the main roof were aflame. With no little difficulty a dozen Brothers hastened down the stairs from roof and tower. Scarcely had they escaped into the open when the whole ceiling fell with a crash, and flames burst out through the broken glass of every window. This was the end of the fine old Hall.

Brother Slattery's courage was equalled by the sympathy he felt for the poor suffering people. One can almost feel his anguish as he described the scene:

Oh, the thousands of wretches in the fields, by the roadsides, starving, half naked, fainting women, crying children, cripples. Oh such a sight of misery. A few hours did it. Water Street & all the merchants' stores destroyed—nothing remains but the extreme west end of the town, Riverhead. Telegrams from Canada & the States promise food & clothing—but who can rebuild our poor town....The sight of a whole town in ruins—say a 1½ mile long by ½ mile wide,—awfully, dreadfully depressing.

But Brother Slattery was not one to wilt under adversity. Grateful to God that the College had survived with its facilities intact, he swiftly organized the staff to offer what relief they could to the suffering people.

Our vacation came before its time. We sent off all the boys as soon as possible, by train & boat and road so as to make room for the homeless creatures on whom God's hand had fallen. From the terrors of that awful night, two of our boys got quite unhinged mentally. One cooled down in good time but the other caused us some anxiety. I sent Br. Baptist [*Flood*] home with him (30 miles). The sight of the old hilltops, the pine woods and his home in their midst calmed him and he is all right now.

In place of our dear boys, the College is almost full, day and night, of men and women, boys and girls. I fear a stranger would not be edified to see the hetero-geneous gathering, but God forbid that we should close the door and refuse shelter to those homeless outcasts crushed by the misfortunes from which we escaped. Our dear Lord opened the wings of his mercy and sheltered us from the destroying angel that, passing by, literally wiped out churches and buildings far more solid and much more valuable than ours. Your heart would bleed to see the thou-sands on thousands of poor creatures huddled by walls and houses, in fields & gardens—anywhere to hid their nakedness and their sorrow. Ten or twelve thousand people so afflicted is a sad sight—but 'tis sadder still to wander among the ruins of our poor town. Its blackened crumbling walls and toppling chimneys make the saddest scene that eye of man can rest upon. From all parts of the world messages full of sympathy and promising supplies have come to soothe our sorrows and heal our wounds. Christianity still rules humanity, for surely only good Christians would have their hearts touched and their purse strings loosed for sorrows so far away from them. The soldiers in Halifax garrison have collected nearly $1000 for our poor people!! the local Gov't sent us to the College unlimited supplies to feed the hungry and they have done the same at the Convents. As all our newspapers have been burned out, you must look to outside publications for a full account....

As I remarked, the College is almost full, especially at night. Poor people can find no roof to cover them. We have reduced things to order. The women of the House look after the females and we see to the other side. Many are very decent people, whose names were always at the head of our Collection list. Some of them and their children we accommodate in the rooms, others in the schools, &.

One incident, a reminder of the very first days of the College, reveals the pathetic plight of so many of the respectable citizens of the town:

Among these fugitives is the Sheriff of the City, an old gentleman named Talbot.[*He was on the Board of Governors of the College.*] About 30 years ago he was professor here under Dr. Mullock and like the hunted hare of Goldsmith he returns again to the old spot....He had no friends, no relatives, no one; he would like to remain with us and die here, above all to be *buried* from the College.

Brother Slattery acceded to Mr. Talbot's request and the latter remained at the College until his death nine years later at the age of ninety.

According to the College Scrap Book, the other "refugees" included Mr. D. J. Greene, Mr. and Mrs. O'Mara, Mr. Cummings, Mr. Foran and family, the Misses Halley, Vinecombe, Joy, and others.

The accumulation of events, not surprisingly, had an impact on Luke's health. His emotional tension is obvious in his handwriting in his letter to the General immediately after the fire. Brother Fleming, Superior of the neighbouring Mount St. Francis community, was so concerned about him that he wrote to the Superior in Ireland that "Poor Br. Luke...spends half the night at times rambling about his room asleep or dreaming and then quite prostrate in the morning. Not able at times for breakfast...he feels a stinging pain at times & a violent palpitation." Apparently Brother Slattery had been troubled with this complaint while in Ireland; now pressures had brought it on again.

But in spite of all life had to go on. In the letter in which he described the effects of the fire, Brother Slattery forwarded his partial financial accounts for the years 1890 and 1891. These showed an income of £1325 for 1890 and £1533 for 1891. He had not yet finished his account of expenditures but estimated that the debt had increased by about £1500. He itemised some of the capital expenditures: "Fences, over £100, Furniture, beds & nearly £600. Repairs, schools, desks, apparatus, besides 4 cows, a horse &." In his defence he emphasised that "these are all permanent and will require no further outlay." He returned to a theme which seems to have been a sore point with him: "When we came here we had not a penny with which to start life. The Bros' rooms, the boys', necessary kitchen arrangements, dining Room & all had to be provided. We had not a book nor knife nor spoon & and then had to begin & prepare a dwelling for more than fifty people." Brother Slattery even found time for a prescient glance towards the future: "I look forward with great pleasure to the day when we shall be able to assume charge of the orphanage."

There were, however, more immediate concerns. Some time previously Brother Slattery and Brother Joseph Crehan had agreed to share in the inspection of the Catholic schools of the island. Shortly after the fire, Brother Crehan set out for Fortune Bay with Brother Andrew Prendergast as companion. Brother Slattery, with young Brother Joseph Culhane for whom the fire must have been a traumatic experience, remained at the College and tried to prepare for the coming year.

CHAPTER SIX

August 1892 – August 1893

Into the Light

*T*he regular exposure of Newfoundlanders to calamities both natural and manmade has given them a remarkable resilience. Even the destruction of St. John's coming so soon after the grim diphtheria epidemic could not defeat them. Like a phoenix from its ashes, the town was soon rising again. Brother Slattery described the bustle in the town at the beginning of November 1892:

> The hum of industry in the rebuilding of the town goes on. On every side the saw and the chisel and the hammer may be heard. Every imaginable form of tilt and shanty, house and store, is exemplified. Much of the work is temporary to be replaced later on. The streets have been straightened considerably and levelled where possible. But many years must pass before the old place will look like itself again.

By Christmas he could report:

> No one would believe the progress made in rebuilding our town. Hundreds of splendid houses have risen as if by the magic effects of a fairy's wand. Certainly one effect of wooden structures is the marvellous quickness with which a house is made ready for occupation. In a few years our town will show little sign of the awful fate that overtook it on July 8th. The streets

are straightened and widened, the old lanes and congested areas opened out, healthy open spaces introduced. All these will give us in a couple of years a much improved and hansomer [sic] town than we had before.

The hope engendered in the people of St. John's by the resurrection of their town was further increased, among the Catholic population particularly, by another event which, though it may seem minor to us now, was of major importance in raising the educational sights of future students and of the people generally. It also provides a revealing glimpse into the sense of social and intellectual inferiority of the Catholic population in respect to their Protestant neighbours, and into the less than ecumenical spirit which prevailed in the country at that time. This event was the announcement in August, 1892 of the results of the London University Matriculation Examination. Brother Slattery's prediction had come true. All four St. Bon's candidates had re-entered into the lists and this time all four had passed, three in the First Division and one in the Second. Francis Connolly, son of Michael Connolly of St. John's, had been awarded the Jubilee Scholarship (£100 a year for two years). The other First Division passes were William Howley, son of James P. Howley, the Geological Surveyor, and Edward P. Roche of Placentia, the future Archbishop. Andrew Jordan, son of James Jordan of St. John's, passed in Second Division. *The Evening Telegram* noted: "Failure in any one subject is enough to prevent the candidate from passing. This fact makes the success of the four St. Bonaventure students the more remarkable; but when it is stated that they are all under 18 years of age it becomes astonishing." The *Telegram* then explained why the College now stood so high in public opinion:

Students of any denomination may enter the College, and there be kindly treated, carefully trained, and not have their religious principles questioned or influenced. They may retire and resume other studies during the expounding of doctrines-they will be simply required to attend lessons on morality, and other teachings necessary to make them honourable sons and creditable citizens. The good Brothers will exercise themselves to advance all students of the College. They will give careful attention to students' morals, health, and intellect....The kind Brothers win their students by love. They extend to them the kindness of parents. Long after the students leave the Brothers' care, in fact, throughout their lives, they cherish thoughts of the happy days spent under them.

Brother Slattery, in describing the success to one of the Assistants in Ireland, summed up his own and the people's reaction to the announcement:

I need not tell you it [*the London Matriculation Exam*] is a very difficult test. Several years have passed since any one even attempted to pass. Well this year, *three* entered from the Wesleyan College and *four* from St. Bonaventure's. When the results were announced it was found that all the Wesleyans had failed and our four poor fellows had come out splendidly, three in the "1st Div." and one in the second. Of course the highest student gets the scholarship for two yrs = $1000. You should know this place, its warm hearted people, and the "*family*" air that pervades their daily intercourse, to understand the enthusiasm and joy that filled the hearts of all our people when the news spread round. It was as if each had made his own fortune. The sneers at the backward state of Catholics, at the retrogressive spirit of our religion, at the degradation of Papists—all were avenged. The Bishop was simply out of himself with joy, and all the priests and—I was going to say all the people—anyway an immense multitude came to congratulate us. As for letters and telegrams—such a shower....Of the four boys, not one is 18 yrs. old while the Wesleyans were 24 and 25, &. Curiously enough, two out of the four go to London to take Degrees in Law, and two others entered All Hallows last week....the Bishop referred most warmly to this "second triumph" of the Bros. here over all the sects. He meant by the 1st. the winning of the Prize Essay.

The success of the College was considered so important that it was noticed overseas. Both the *Dublin Freeman's Journal* and *The Irish Catholic* published articles congratulating the school. The *Freeman*, contrasting the situation in Newfoundland with that prevailing in Ireland, commented:

Each and every body and institution [*in Newfoundland*] is free to follow its own methods and system subject, of course, to an education Government inspection, which however, does not, as here at home, imply the banishment from the classroom of every religious emblem or picture. The result of this is that the Catholics, having a free field and no favour, can show not only their desire for thorough education, but also the remarkable success which attends their efforts....

The school year was off to a good start. So was the fledgling novitiate. Two of the four candidates had left during the summer but their places had been taken by four others.

Brother Slattery had been concerned that the disastrous fire would mean a considerable reduction in the numbers of his pupils but he found his roll almost up to scratch, possibly because St. Patrick's Hall Schools, whose classrooms had burned down, were being conducted in temporary quarters and the parents who could afford it preferred to enroll them at St. Bon's. The academic success of the College would also have encouraged them. By Christmas numbers rose to eighty day boys and forty boarders, including twelve normals.

On September 21, Brother Calasanctius Whitty, Assistant to the Superior General, arrived in St. John's to inspect the Brothers' schools. In his Report to the Superior, Brother Whitty noted that diphtheria was still in the city, that one of the boys at the College had got the disease but had been immediately removed to hospital and was recovering while one of the boys in Holy Cross had died of it during the previous week. Regarding the Brothers he stated: "The Brs. here are certainly in high favour with all—Bp., priests & people. They are respected, beloved and admired." One extraordinary proof of this last statement was the annual collection for the support of the Brothers at Mount St. Francis. It was naturally expected that, with much of the town in ruins, the collection would be down considerably, but in fact it amounted to $2060, the largest since the Brothers had set foot on the island.

In November, with the school now settled down again, Brother Slattery made his postponed inspection tour of the outport schools, principally to the island of Oderin which he found to be a fascinating but very wearying experience.

The part I had to visit stretches along about seventy miles & when I tell you that there are not five miles of road in all that you can understand the facilities of travelling. The little schools are few and far apart, the settlements isolated and lonely, the people poor and primitive....Nearly all the travelling has to be done in open boats, generally to beg shelter from the inclemency of a cold November night. I was a thousand times welcome to the best they had, but the musty bed, the rancid butter, the fishy odours, the wretched surroundings were poor substitutes for the pure, if bitter, breezes of the open sea. With two guides, next morning, I reached my destination. Such a road!! Over the wild barrens, across a trackless morass or through a miry bog—I never suffered such torture. You may remember a famous toe [*injury referred to in a previous letter*]. Every step of that weary five miles, over those pathless bogs and rocks sent a thrill of pain from one

47

of my extremities—literally—to the other. Multiply these experiences by a fortnight and you may guess how glad I was to reach home again.

On his return he was kept busy supervising the examination for teachers which had been established under the new regulations.

The College now had a new property, given to it by a Miss Delaney who had owned the house and observatory just across the street from the College. Brother Slattery was delighted; the income from this house could be used to support the novitiate. This house, though no longer the property of the College, is still in excellent condition.

With no new crisis to attend to, Brother Slattery could take the opportunity to look outside the College to the events of the city. At Christmas, he noted:

Just as I write, the "S. S. Kite" is entering the "Narrows" having on board the Polar Expedition party under Lieutenant Peary. They have spent the winter on the extreme north coast of Greenland. They are all safe and it is said have made most valuable additions to the knowledge of Arctic life. Their object was not to reach the pole itself, but to take observations.

In contrast to previous years, the problems during this year were very minor ones. A very severe winter lasting into May, coupled with burst pipes, was the worst the College could complain about. In May Brother Slattery reported that he had rented a farm belonging to Dr. Howley's brother. There were twenty-six acres at a rent of $160 or about £21 a year. He hoped to save money by raising vegetables and milk cows there.

In the same letter, Brother Slattery explained how, with the cooperation of the Headmasters of the other Colleges, he succeeded in having the government allot money for prizes, etc. for competition between the schools.

The Head Teacher of the Prot. [*Anglican*] College and myself are good friends. He is a very upright honest Englishman and was one of the first to call and offer his congratulations last year. Speaking with him lately I regretted the apathy that hung over educational matters, having no competition, no life, no soul, in any department. He brought the Head of the Wesleyan College next day. The three of us waited on the three Supts. of Education and they agreed to accompany us in a deputation to the Govt. The Cabinet, or as we call it here, the Executive, received us most kindly and the heads of a Bill were agreed to, at once. We expected about $1000 a year and to secure it asked for $2000. The Executive was so impressed by our advocacy that it gave $4000 without any demur. This expended judiciously will put great life in the higher classes. Diplomas, prizes and a few small scholarships are the means by which the work is to be done.

The Distribution of Prizes in July was followed next day by a sports day and both were very successful. Brother Slattery concluded the year by saying, "Our prospects at the College were never brighter and with God's blessing we shall avail of the sunshine." Unfortunately the sunshine was soon to become overclouded again.

First C.H.E. Exam in Bishop's Library, 1894

CHAPTER SEVEN

September 1893 – July 1894

The Clouds Return

*T*he 1893-4 school year started off as buoyantly as had its predecessor. Following up the triumphant success of the previous year, the College had entered two candidates for the London Matriculation Examination in July 1893. *The Evening Telegram* told the story:

> The young gentlemen who have finished these examinations are Mr. John Sullivan and Mr. T. L. Greene, from Saint Bonaventure, and Mr. Cowperthwaite from the Wesleyan College. All three have been trained under experienced and clever teachers, those from St. Bonaventure's College having studied under the Rev. Brother Crehan, who has already successfully trained four candidates in Newfoundland, besides others in Ireland. Mr Cowperthwaite received his training from Professor Holloway, a gentleman well known for his learning and ability. The result of the examinations will not be known for some months, as the papers will have to undergo a rigid examination in London, where the least flaw or mistake will be recognized, and when we hope there will come three certificates, awarding places in the first division to Newfoundland's competitors in the great field of education... [*In 1891*] the examinations were excessively hard and all the students failed, but since then four diplomas have been awarded successful

students from Saint Bonaventure's College, which has taken the lead in this respect, and we hope to see those exams patronized every year. Thus the great cause of education will advance in Newfoundland to the standard it has reached in the mother country.

When the results of these exams were published in September, it was found that John Sullivan, who had entered the novitiate the year previously as Brother Benedict, had not only passed in First Division but had achieved the highest mark that had ever been received in Newfoundland although he was only sixteen years of age when he took the exam. It appears that Cowperthwaite, the first student from Wesleyan College to matriculate, also passed but "far behind" Sullivan, and that the other St. Bon's candidate did not pass.

In July also, forty-six normals and teachers had taken the Grade exams "before Inspector Wickham in the Episcopal Library," and had done well. On October 1, a young man of twenty-six, who had been teaching for six years, entered the novitiate. He was Patrick Strapp from Harbour Main who, as Brother Vincent, was to be synonymous with the College for many years until his death there in 1952.

But before the new year came in, the College was to see the sudden death of its main supporter, Bishop Power, and the near death of Brother Slattery himself. Brother Slattery may have had a premonition of this when he wrote to Brother Whitty in December 1892: "Everything goes on well with us still. I daresay our clouds will gather again as they did three years ago! We had a sad Xmas then with a houseful of patients. But it's gone."

In October a neglected cold resulted in Brother Slattery's catching a severe case of diphtheria, which necessitated his being taken to the Fever Hospital on Signal Hill. He told the story in his own inimitable style and in doing so painted a graphic picture of this now forgotten institution.

...Well here I am again in the clutches of Diphtheria.
A heavy cold, somewhat neglected I must say, acted
the janitor and our old enemy stole in. Though my
throat seemed quite *full* of the usual membranous
matter and my whole neck enflamed and stiff yet mine
is not a very severe case. After four or five days the
soreness softened and I was able to swallow something. Thank God, I am the only sufferer this time. It
is strange how Providence reminds us of life's brevity
and of our slender hold on it, just when we are
inclined to forget? Our nos. increased daily till we had
51 boarders and nearly 100 day boys. We had to open
another class room for the juniors and all seemed
joyous and auspicious. Then I had to lie down and I
knew our old visitor too well to be decieved [*sic*] in the
symptoms. Next day the Doctor had to come—of
course there was no doubt...

I have been much more sick than the Bros. knew—I
had no heart to give the poor fellows bad news when
they came outside to ask for me. Not being able to see
them was the hardest part. I have told them I would
be home early next week—but I think this letter will
be with you before I see them.

I daresay you forget where *this* hospital is. You
remember the Block House, high over the "Narrows," from which signals are made of incoming
vessels. Well the Diphtheria Hospital is just under the
Block House-right over the sea. From my bed I can
see the wild rolling waters below, and the fishing boats
tossing around as they gather the precarious harvest
of the sea. Off and on, a large steamer breaks the
monotony and pushes its way through-a messenger
from afar. A few nights ago quite a heavy storm raged
and a Norwegian barque was wrecked right under the
Hospital—not 200 yds. away. The signals of distress

were sad and painful in the silence & the storm of midnight. Blazing torches, with the booming of a cannon left no doubt on a listener's mind that it was a "wild night at sea." Thro the bravery of our pilots 12 out of 14 men were saved. The other two had travelled far to find a watery shroud. There is a fireside far away in a Norwegian valley where perhaps their names are murmured affectionately tonight, but they will never see the wild Fiords of their Northern home again.

All day long I look out at the wild sea below me. I count the fishing boats and follow with my eyes, the calm flight of the sea gulls. I listen to the never ceasing boom of the waters. You won't be astonished to learn that sometimes my eyes wander farther seaward and across all the miles of water, towards the "Fair Hills of Holy Ireland". I dare say sickness makes the exile's heart a little softer than usual.

This old building is not without interest. It was raised by the French during their occupation, and still bears traces of its architects. I have a whole ward to myself and over my bed are the iron brackets for holding the carbines in place. There they are in each corner. These quaint irons stood out there long before Wolfe and Montcalm met on the heights of Quebec! The French sentinel's "Qui vive?" rang out here under these windows. The gay *chansons* of Normandy and Britanny made this very room resound with joy as the revellers remembered the vineyards of old France. The hearthstone is an Iron shutter!! Over an inch thick it tells of the troublous times when the occupants of this place felt secure behind its protecting folds. But high up on Signal Hill the Union Jack now calmly tells the stranger, far out at sea, that the "Lilies of France" no longer floats over "La Terre Neuve" of these days. That banner went down on the "Plains of Abraham"....

I must acknowledge I felt lonely and sad at spending the 18th. [*the feast day of St. Luke*] in the ward of an

Hospital without seeing face of one Br!! It was the darkest Feast I ever spent—but it is over and I am out of danger. So, thanks be to God who is so good to us all.

On Monday, October 23, Brother Slattery, though still very weak, was well enough to return to the College, much to the relief of Brother Baptist Flood who had been in charge during his absence, and whose delicate state of health was endangered by the pressures of responsibility. But hardly had he returned when he received a severe blow from a most unexpected direction. Brother Joseph Crehan had written to the Superior complaining of his irritability, saying that "he was at times almost unapproachable," that he had no time for class because he was so engaged in other activities, and revealing his own lack of comprehension of the multiplicity of problems that confronted Brother Slattery by stating: "after all there's not so much work in the management of the establishment!" The Superior General, without checking further, wrote severely to Brother Slattery about those matters.

Brother Slattery reacted characteristically. It was the custom for the Brothers after evening prayers on Friday nights to accuse themselves before the community of faults they might have committed during the week against the Rule or against their Brothers. On the Friday night after receiving the Superior's reprimand, Brother Slattery knelt before the community, read to them the Superior's letter and apologised for the bad example he had given them; he did this although, as he afterwards wrote to Brother Whitty, one of the Assistants to the General:

Had I been accused of sheep stealing I could not be more stunned than when I recently received a letter from Br. Superior telling me that I should "restrain my temper" and that I was "so irritable at times" that the "Brothers would not come near" me. Well honestly, I have not Job's patience, but in the days of my deepest contrition I never dreamed I was such a tyrant that the "Brothers would not come near" me.

The other Brothers in the community were equally stunned. They vigorously disagreed with Brother Crehan's view and wasted no time in informing the Superior accordingly. Brother Andrew Prendergast wrote: "I beg to state here that in my experience with Br. Luke, I always found him just the reverse to what you have come to hear about him." And Brother Joseph Culhane was more emphatic.

I think there must have been some mistake, for kindness to others, especially to the Brothers, is characteristic of him. If he were accused of being too indulgent, I could understand it; but I thought even an enemy could not accuse him of being unapproachable....He has never once treated me harshly during the three years I have been with them, and when I want anything I have no hesitation in going to him.

Some time later Brother Slattery received what amounted to a letter of apology from the Superior for his rather hasty rebuke. One good result of this episode was that it brought out the true nature of the regard the Brothers as a whole had for Brother Slattery. Nor did he bear any resentment towards Brother Crehan for his complaint. In May 1894 he wrote to the Superior asking permission for Brothers Crehan and Prendergast to holiday in Ireland during the summer: "These good Brothers deserve every favour the Institute can confer on them...these good Brothers deserve this thing as they have built up this College and, more than any one else, contributed to its success." Here was magnanimity in action!

Brother Crehan was soon to change his mind about the requirements of running the College. On Brother Slattery's retirement in the summer of 1896, Brother Crehan was appointed College President. Even before school had started in September, he broke down and had to be recalled to Ireland.

In November 1893, Brother Slattery could report that there were almost 150 students on the roll, including forty-nine boarders and four novice Brothers in training. But shortly after, all plans were upset by the unexpected death of Bishop Power on December 4. Brother Slattery, in particular, was much affected by the loss of a great friend and supporter. As he reported to Brother Whitty in Ireland:

> ...we were all so distracted about the poor Bishop that we forgot everything....He had been depressed for some time—sickish, &—but nothing seriously wrong. Then came a heavy cold, not attended to, and all was over in a day....He was a man of great and simple faith....Coming here 23 yrs ago he brought with him some of the sentiments then common among the Dublin priests regarding the Bros. Little by little his honesty of heart showed him the true worth of the Bros. work and from being a cold official he became an ardent friend. Friend! no words can express his childish affection for some of us. The success of the College was, he said, the crowning glory of his pastoral life....The day I went to Hospital, he did not taste a morsel from morning till night....When I returned he came and sat beside me for hours at a time and when leaving invariably settled the bed clothes round me—a mother could not be more tender to her child.

Evidence of the cordial relations between the Bishop and the Brothers was that the latter were the chief mourners at his funeral, walking immediately behind the coffin and in front of the clergy. The appointment of a new bishop was awaited with great "fear and trembling" since some of the names mentioned were of a very different stamp. As it turned out, the question of who would be the new bishop would not be answered until February 1895.

Whatever else changed, one thing that remained constant was the need to deal with the College debt. In the new year, Brother Slattery began remote preparations for holding a bazaar during the following autumn in order to reduce the debt, which now amounted to over £3000.

The island was undergoing its worst winter in many years. "Mountains of snow!!" Brother Slattery noted, " I never saw more....Yesterday I walked straight from the College across our fence, the road, and the Bros' fence, to Mt. St. Francis. Indeed there was little sign of fence or road." Soon he was sick again, this time with a severe case of la grippe. *The Evening Telegram* of January 15, 1894 reported it thus:

> GRIPPE IN THE COLLEGE.—The Rev. President, Brother Slattery, and sixteen students of St. Bonaventure's College are prostrated with la grippe. Mr. Slattery has had a pretty sharp attack, but is improving, and in most cases among the students the touch has been light.

Not only was the winter severe, it was very long. Even at the beginning of May, according to Brother Slattery's account, there was:

> ...not a blade of grass, not a leaf nor a bud, nothing but snow and ice. The country is still white, only the hill sides, rocks & prominent spots are bare. The whole coast is blocked with a boundless field of ice. Several steamers are lying off the coast, waiting for an opening to make a dash for port. It is really the longest, dreariest winter since I came here.

Brother Slattery wrote this letter while lying in bed recovering from another bout of diphtheria. At the same time Mr. Talbot, the College's permanent guest since the 1892 fire, was anointed and the worst was feared, though in fact he recovered and lived until 1901.

Meanwhile the competition for scholastic success was heating up with both the Jubilee Scholarship and the new Council of Higher Education (CHE) scholarships and prizes now up for competition. Since this was the first time the scholastic standing of the various schools could be directly compared, feelings naturally ran high. Brother Slattery's letter to Brother Whitty reveals how involved the whole community was in the results.

Today begins the Matric. Exam. for the big scholarship ($960). The Wesleyans are sending on five, the Protestants *one* and St. Bonaventure's two (Howley & Strapp). The odds are against us. The Protestant has been four years grinding and is, as well as most of the Methodists, nearly twenty years of age. Our two have just reached sixteen—the minimum age. But we have every Nun and other pious person in the Island praying for us. Some of us never prayed so fervently before. Surely our dear Lord will hear us! David never went forth against Goliath with more faith and trust in the Lord than does poor Harry Strapp go into this Exam. He feels as if the whole Catholic Church had put into his hands, its cause and its honour.

On June 11 the London University Matriculation Examination began with its eight competitors, and on the June 25, the CHE commenced with 950 entries in two grades, Senior for students under seventeen years of age and Junior for those under fifteen. St. Bon's had seventy-five entries. For the supervision of these exams, Brother Slattery and Mr. Blackall of the Wesleyan College changed places. Brother Slattery noted that "for the past week I have had entire charge of the Protestant boys and girls and of all their exams. I must say I have found them very honorable and honest. Not the remotest attempt at foul play or the like." As a humorous aside he added, "You won't mind that this is written with *Protestant ink* nor that I am surrounded by about sixty Protestant boys & girls!!!"

The importance of the exams to the intellectual level of the country was highlighted by an article in *The Evening Telegram* of July 2. It stated:

At nearly thirty centres, in different parts of the Island, the first examination by the Council of Higher Education commenced last Monday...nearly a thousand young aspirants have trooped out to enter the lists for their first tournament of life. Episcopalian,

Catholic and Wesleyan, sit side by side in this juvenile contest for first place....Hitherto each denomination has adopted its own methods and followed its own plans. Without doubt much has been done, often under circumstances very adverse. But it was only natural to slacken the pace when there was no competition, that the waters should become stagnant when there was no motion. The dry rot of dullness and apathy was fast eating its way into the very heart of our educational machinery. But as if an electric current had passed, the new system has put spirit and life in the classrooms, and energy and diligence are exercising their beneficent influence. The dry branches that seemed dead have put forth buds and flowers, and a bounteous vintage may be expected.

The *Telegram* emphasised also the social and political improvement that it was hoped the new exams would bring about:

The moral and social effect of having so many hundreds of our boys and girls of all classes and denominations so competing in youthful emulation is beyond all calculation. That very sectarian spirit which in the years past caused so much turmoil and disorder, so much injustice and misery, is here utilized in a blessed manner for mutual good, and for the general benefit of our people. It looks as if the vexed problem of centuries might be solved by our children.

While waiting for the results to be announced, the College held the annual sports day, a great success with about 4,000 people present including the Governor and Lady O'Brien as well as the Commodore and all the officers of the war ships which were visiting St. John's. Never one to miss an opportunity, Brother Slattery arranged with the Commodore for a "Grand Military Tournament, Assault at Arms, &" at the College in aid of the bazaar.

Brothers Prendergast and Crehan had been permitted to return to Ireland for a vacation during the summer and, in spite of all his activity, Brother Slattery found himself very lonely. He wrote to Brother Whitty:

> I wish I could exchange with either of these good Bros. so that I might see some old friends again. Ah, dear! how green the hills seem and how fair the valleys are, when viewed in the dreams of the poor exile!! And how true are the friends and how fond are the Bros. when reflected on by foreign shores!!

Meanwhile there was other business to attend to. At the end of July, Brother Slattery was in Harbour Grace. Far from the green hills of his musings, the exile was busy supervising the examinations of the student-teachers there. Thus ended another school year.

Students on College campus c. 1900

CHAPTER EIGHT

August 1894 – July 1895

Triumph and Tragedy

*E*ven during vacation time Brother Slattery did not seem able to escape drama. Two incidents during August 1894, one humorous, the other tragic, reveal both his sympathy with the down-and-out and his influence with the powers-that-be. Here are the stories in his own words:

Last week passing one of the streets I saw a policeman ill treat a poor drunken man. I stopped him and got the poor man to go quietly. What was my astonishment next morning to learn that the poor man had received a sentence of 100 days imprisonment for assaulting a policemen!! I at once drove out to the country where the Judge (Prowse, a Protestant) lived. I told him the injustice he had done & and expostulated with him. "Well, what do you want me to do?" he said, "To release him at once," I answered. He got his hat, came back with me and let out the poor man that same evening. Some one asked him why he had released the man. "Why if Mr. Slattery asked me to let out every prisoner in the jail I could not refuse him", he answered. But to the Inspector of Police, who felt aggrieved, he gave a different reason. "If I refused him," said he, "he would go at once to the Governor and 'Terry' would do anything for Slattery." 'Terry' is a friendly nickname some people here have for the Governor—Sir Terence [*O'Brien*].

Another day, a story appeared in the local newspapers that Brother Slattery had been assaulted by a maniac. According to Brother Slattery himself:

It is all a story as far as I was concerned tho' an awful affair in itself. He was just landed from a steamer, was drunk, got annoyed at some boys who chaffed him, etc., drew a knife on them. They ran away. Seeing me he wanted to complain the boys. To show them what he would do to them he had gashed all his arm. He was so beastly drunk, and so covered with blood, I turned into a shop. Now for the end—an awful one. He was taken to hospital; he swore so much that Dr. Shea expostulated. "I'll be in Hell in 24 hours," he answered. He was a Catholic and, without priest or Sacraments, died during the night. He was a murderer and had been sentenced to be hanged but got reprieved. The poor fellow meant me no harm, but I cannot help shivering when I remember his awful death.

The school year opened quietly with Brother Slattery busy preparing for the bazaar he was planning to hold to help pay off some of the school debt. Both St. Bon's candidates in the London University Matriculation Exams had passed. They were Alex Howley and Harry Strapp. The Jubilee Scholarship, however, had gone to Ralph Wood of The Church of England College, a not unexpected result since Wood was nineteen while the College hopeful, Harry Strapp, was only sixteen.

Then at the beginning of October the long awaited results of the CHE exams were published. And what a triumph they were for the College and for Brother Slattery. He had expected good results but, as he said, "my wildest dreams ne'er rose to a hope of the reality that has come." St. Bon's had won eight of the ten scholarships offered, with the Church of England College and St. Patrick's Hall getting the other two. Of the special prizes—English, Latin, etc.—the College had won twenty-nine, the other two colleges seven each. Fifty-eight St. Bon's boys had passed, compared with forty-six from

Church of England College and forty from Wesleyan College. Among the St. Bon's students who were prize winners in senior grade were such later well-known figures as William Kitchen and Vincent Burke; while in junior grade appeared the names of John Fenelon, Richard Howley, Edward English and George Kearney.

In our more sophisticated age, it is difficult to appreciate the excitement among the people which the publishing of these results evoked. Brother Slattery was almost beside himself with joy: "Never since Jacques Cartier laid his eyes on these rocky shores has the Catholic Church won such a victory here. Our people are simply delirious over this grand result." He described the scene which ensued when he and Brother Crehan arrived home after assisting in compiling the results, with the final marks tabulated at four o'clock in the morning.

> We reached home before five o'clock, called the others and laughed and shouted and roared till six o'clock when I went to bed. How the next day passed I know not. Waterloo brought less joy to London than did our great victory call forth to our good Catholics of St. John's. Crowds, telegrams, letters, &. Why it is beyond description.

And yet he could not help remembering the one who was missing:

> Ah, but the broken string!! the sad remembrance! He who would weep with joy was not there. Our own dear Bishop and father was not with us on this great day. Immense as are the joys of heaven I am sure he was happier at knowing what occurred. When I spoke of this to poor Fr. Scott [*the administrator at the Cathedral*] he simply cried like a child.

Some idea of the enlarged opportunities which the new educational system had opened up for the students can be gained from following the later careers of the prize winners. Ralph Wood, for instance, graduated from Cambridge University and later became the first native Headmaster of Bishop Feild College; William Kitchen became a priest, obtained his Doctorate in Divinity from Louvain University, and served the St. John's archdiocese for many years, ending as its Vicar General with the title of Monsignor; Vincent Burke became R.C. Superintendent of Education and later Deputy Minister, served as the first Chairman of the Board of Memorial University, of which he is considered one of the founders. Many of the other winners also obtained high positions in state and church both in Newfoundland and elsewhere.

Unfortunately this scholastic success had an unexpectedly adverse affect in another area—the bazaar. The other denominations were naturally shocked at the extent of their defeat and were less enthusiastic than usual in helping the Brothers. One can understand why in the light of their own financial obligations:

> This year the C. of E. College went $23,000 in debt and the Wesleyans laid out $50,000 in rebuilding theirs which the fire destroyed. Our debt then seems small and they say "If such things happen in the green woods, what might they expect in the dry".

Other factors came into play as well. After the death of Bishop Power there was intense controversy in the local Church as to whom his successor should be. A year previously Bishop Power had been given an auxiliary, a Bishop Brennan, previously the first Bishop of Dallas, Texas, a position he had left in controversial circumstances. He was very popular with a certain faction in St. John's who strongly supported his appointment, while others, particularly the clergy, who knew his unsuitability, were vehemently opposed. Since the priests were doing all they could to help the bazaar, the admirers of Bishop Brennan refused to take any part in it at all, particularly when they heard that the Bishop had not been asked to open the Bazaar.

The Brothers had always steered away from any political involvement; still events in that arena also influenced the situation. The two political parties, the Liberals and the Tories, were bitterly opposed to each other, so much so that according to a contemporary, Judge Prowse, "...in their mad desire for revenge on each other true patriotism disappeared, and the vital interests of our unfortunate Colony were entirely ignored." Brother Slattery, reporting the event afterwards, shows how complicated affairs in a small town can be:

No Bazaar ever had so many mountains to climb. We selected the very best weeks in which to hold it and our blessed Tory Government selected the *last* of these weeks in which to hold the elections....Then *some* said the Bros. in general were Tories, but Mr. Slattery was so in particular. Others whispered— "not at all, every one of them was a Liberal—a Whitewayite," etc., etc. We were accused even of having canvassed during Vacation. So politics injured us, though I may tell you there was not a particle of foundation.

Still, in spite of all the obstacles, the bazaar didn't do too badly. In all, the College cleared almost $6000— about half of what Brother Slattery had originally hoped for. And it was well that it did, for soon disaster struck the city.

For some time there had been rumours that all was not well with the finances of the island. For several years the cod fishery, on which the whole economy of the island depended, had been in decline. The merchants, who were also the directors of the banks, had borrowed heavily and greatly overdrawn their accounts to maintain the credit of their establishments. Then a partner of one of the large fish-exporting firms died and his associates refused to continue "accepting exchanges" until an investigation of their accounts had been made. This one act brought the whole intricate financial system down like a house of cards. On "Black Monday," December 10, 1894, the two banks, the Union Bank of Newfoundland and the Commercial Bank, were forced to suspend operations. With no money in circulation, business came to a standstill and workmen were dismissed wholesale. A Royal Commission in 1933 reported the result:

> Bread riots arising out of the distress took place at St. John's. Crowds first surrounded the House of Assembly demanding "food or work." On returning, they attacked a store and pillaged its contents. Sailors and marines were landed to protect public property.

Judge Prowse, writing in the immediate aftermath of the bank crash, sadly noted:

> For several days we were the most distracted country in the world. A community without a currency; the notes of the banks had been the universal currency of the Colony—circulating as freely as gold on Saturday, on Monday degraded to worthless paper.

Though it is agreed that "reckless banking" was the immediate cause of the disaster, Prowse placed the fundamental blame on "the fierce rancour and bitter personal hate which characterised their [merchants and politicians] party struggles."

Amid this climate of "fierce rancour" and bitter personal hate, Brother Slattery, remaining aloof from all such party politics, managed to maintain the respect and friendship of all groups. Nevertheless, in spite of his deep love for Newfoundland, he was not blind to her many foibles and follies. Judge Prowse had given as the only possible explanation of the debacle, the old saying: "Whom the gods wish to destroy, they first make mad." Brother Slattery put the matter somewhat more pungently:

> This is a most extraordinary country. It always does extraordinary things in a most extraordinary way. We had a prince for a bishop, no one wanted him, no one

liked him. An unknown stranger (Dr. Brennan) comes along and everyone falls down to *adore* him. Other places have fires, we go and burn the *Capital* to the ground. Our Commons refuse a Revenue Bill and Duties are collected by force of arms without any Law to authorize the act. We are always singing "God save the Queen," yet *not a man* will enlist in Army or Navy. A bank closes—there is no circulating medium. It is a novel experience to find a whole people without currency—but enough.

And again:

In this poor Colony *credit* has been their God. The fishermen went in debt to the planter, the planter to the merchant, the merchant to the Banks, the Banks to the Govt. (Savings Bank), the Govt. to money lenders abroad. One brick fell from the building and the mighty edifice of the God Credit fell immediately.

He is scathing in his comments about the management of one of the banks:

The directors of the Commercial overdrew their own a/c's to more than five times the value of the entire stock!! It was a huge swindle. Each endorsed the Bills of the others and an immense business—on paper—was carried on.

His sympathy for the people who had suffered so greatly shows through in his lament that "an Arctic winter is on us and hundreds, thousands of people are after being ruined." He described the impact of the crash on the public:

Our financial collapse is far more serious than the fire which wiped out three fourths of the city. The saddest feature is the sight of decent families, reduced to penury. Money was easily made in the old times. Many a poor Irish Emigrant, unable to write his name, landed here made money, invested it in the banks and died leaving his family in opulence. His grandchildren are now poorer than he was when he landed. They are worse—he was able to work, they are not. Of course the fisheries are there still, an overflowing spring of wealth. but it will take a long time to reconstitute business habits and set the wheels in motion.

But he could be critical of the ordinary people too:

There is much poverty and hunger but it is accompanied by more laziness and idleness. I have often noticed a spirit of fatalism in the people here. Under sorrow and affliction they sit down in the dull apathy of despair or simply float away on the wave of misfortune that threatens them, making little effort to overcome their trials. Neither the wail of sorrow, the cry of defiance, much less the hearty shout of manly hope—no, the storm has come, the vessel must be lost, we can do no more. Well, no doubt the shadows that hang over us are heavy and are enough to unnerve even more heroic hearts.

Once more Brother Slattery was not content just to sit back and lament the misfortune that had befallen the country. Perhaps nothing could illustrate better the acuteness of his mind and his influence over his fellow citizens than the following incident narrated years later by one of his fellow Brothers.* On the failure of the two banks, the government had hurriedly passed a bill guaranteeing the notes of the banks at 80% of their face value in the case of the Union Bank and only 20% in that of the Commercial Bank.

---

* It can be found in the 1927 issue of *The Christian Brothers Educational Record.* p.228f. The author is unknown, possibly Br. Joseph Crehan.

It is difficult to realize the confusion and distress that prevailed throughout the Colony at this time. Most people had been investing all their saving in bank shares, which had been paying twenty to twenty-five per cent. in dividends notwithstanding repeated "waterings." Fortunately, many held Government debentures; except for these debentures the whole reserve of the business community, the whole savings of many a life-time, suddenly vanished.

Somebody at last suggested that the Government should guarantee the full face value of all the notes and make them legal tender. This idea spread like wild-fire; especially was it favoured by note-holders of the Commercial Bank, who were in sore straits. The Cabinet were in a serious dilemma. The proposal was fraught with the direst danger to the credit of the Colony, but in face of the gathering force of public opinion, what were they to do? The merchants were in a state of trepidation. Was the Colony on the brink of financial ruin?

Br. Luke gave some days to deep study of the currency question....Finally, he concluded calmly and judicially that the proposal before the Cabinet would, if accepted, be disastrous. He had a marvellously clear mind, and, as a consequence, a rare lucidity of exposition, and a style that was classic in its strength and simplicity. Never did he use these rare gifts to better effect than in the long letter which, one memorable day, appeared over his name in the columns of the two newspapers published daily in St. John's.* The whole morning the chamber of Commerce had been in anxious deliberation. Suddenly a latecomer dashed into the council chamber, newspaper in hand. He announced the publication of a letter from Br. Slattery, and without waiting to sit down read it to an

---

* January 10, 1895. The full letter can be found in Appendix 3.

excited but spell-bound audience. Evidently the last word was said; such was the opinion of all present. On the conclusion of the reading of the letter everyone jumped to his feet and cheered again and again for Br. Slattery. The account of the scene was related to one of the Brothers by the Protestant merchant who had thus read the letter.

And the cause was ended. No more was heard of a forced currency. Members of the Cabinet expressed their relief and gratitude in private letters to Br. Luke. The ablest lawyer in St. John's at that time was Alexander MacNeilly.... His closely-written letter complimenting Br. Luke on his manifesto—it was nothing less—ran to thirty-two pages of letter paper.

St. Paul tells us that lest the greatness of the revelations he had received should make him proud, he was given "a sting of the flesh" to keep him humble. Now, in the midst of his success, Brother Slattery was to receive a similar "sting."

Unexpectedly the trouble was to come from his own religious community. It would appear that during the previous summer vacation, Brother Flood had written to the Superior General asking for a transfer from the College "for the sake of his soul." Brother Flood was a very sensitive, scrupulous individual and was upset about the apparent lack of regularity in the prayer life of the St. Bon's community. After a discussion with Brother Slattery he had changed his, mind. Though his second letter has not survived, it would appear that shortly after the bazaar he wrote to the Superior again, this time in an even more critical vein. The Superior removed him to Mount St. Francis—much to the loss of the College—and wrote a scathing letter to Brother Slattery pointing out the many presumed defects in his conduct of the community, mainly in the regularity of the community prayer life, and warning that he "could not allow the Novitiate there to continue as things have been." This letter must have been a tremendous shock to Brother Slattery, but his reply shows both greatness and humility. He began by acknowledging the justice of much of the criticism:

First of all, I am sure you will believe me when I say that I regret exceedingly at being the cause of so much anxiety and trouble to you. You have ever been kind to me, considerate of my weaknesses and exaggerating any good I may have done. Even with the serious list of offences mentioned in your letter there is no word of bitterness and little to show the annoyance you must necessarily feel. For all this, as I say, I am not ungrateful.

I might write you a long letter of explanation on those various matters, and I could say much on each, but I shall start by telling you candidly that, on the whole, what you say is not far removed from a correct statement of the facts. I might explain this point and give reasons for that but what would be the good! I presume your object is the mending of what is amiss and not a discussion as to the varying extent of my carelessness on these various points. Of my immediate attention to these irregularities you may be certain, and where things can be improved I shall leave nothing undone to succeed.

He then explained that most of these problems arose during the preparation for and the running of the bazaar, and rather casually mentioned the enormous amount of supervision connected with the running of a boarding school, not to mention the conduct of the College itself. He defended the conduct of the novices, pointing out their excellent record. Finally he wrote:

And now, my most dear Br. Superior, I come to the last point, and this has been in no way affected by your last letter. For many months I have determined that when the Bazaar had closed I should place my resignation in your hands...I feel the time has come for an abler hand to guide this College. I resign it then into your hands convinced more than ever that it has a useful and brilliant career before it. I thank you most heartily for all the kindness you have shown me at all times and the toleration you have extended towards my many shortcomings. And having resigned the College and its direction, I now resign myself. I place myself at your disposal absolutely. If you think me more fitted for a kitchen than for a school I am at your entire disposal. For thirty years I have been more or less an unprofitable subject in the Institute. May the years that remain be more fruitful. But again, I would ask you not to associate this with your letter—there is no connection. Speaking of our Boarders here the Br. Assistant when on Visitation said that they seemed more like a religious community than a crowd of boys. Whoever takes my place will find the same still,—he will find also a community of Bros. as efficient, as assiduous and as edifying as any in the Institute.

The fact is, that great as were the ability and energy of Brother Slattery, the multiplicity of tasks that he had undertaken was beyond the capacity of any one man, no matter how gifted. When his eventual successor, Brother Bernard Lavelle, arrived on the scene, he was not long in complaining to the Superior of the impossible task that had been given him.

Shortly after the bank crash, one good piece of news was announced. St. John's was finally to have a new bishop. He was Bishop Michael F. Howley, Vicar Apostolic of St. George's. Of all the likely candidates, Bishop Howley was the one whom Brother Slattery much preferred. He was an ex-pupil of St. Bon's, having been a member of its first class while it was still located in the Old Palace on Theatre Hill, and had always been very friendly towards the Brothers. He arrived in February and quickly assured the Brothers of his friendship and confirmed their use of the "Bishop's Farm" which his predecessor had allowed for the use of the College.

Because of the financial troubles of the island, the College lost some of its students, but their numbers remained relatively high, about 140 towards the end of the year. While other religious houses lost heavily in the aftermath of the bank crash, St. Bon's emerged comparatively unscathed, losing only about $500. Brother Slattery proposed to take advantage of the situation to obtain a lower rate on the College debt by borrowing from the government at the reduced rate and paying off the bank. For some complicated financial reason, this scheme seems to have had advantages for all concerned. But it did not eventuate since the Superiors in Ireland viewed the scheme with scepticism.

And so another school year came to an end with public examinations and sports day. The Superior General wrote Brother Slattery suggesting that he might come back to Ireland for a holiday. Although he was thrilled at the possibility, Brother Slattery reluctantly declined, believing it would be wrong to do so when so many people in the city were facing such great economic hardships.

The year ended more brightly than had seemed possible a few months earlier. Both the seal catch and the cod fishery were highly successful and the economy began to recover. The Brothers received a valuable new addition when a boarder, Patrick McCarthy from Northern Bay, entered the novitiate.

In spite of all the problems of the year, Brother Slattery savoured the little things in life, and we have to smile at his words written at the end of June:

> We had a great treat today at dinner—we had turnip tops!! Now you may laugh but after seven months without a fresh vegetable one is easily pleased. All our vegetables stored since last October are a little stale. Cabbage is here now—brought from New York, 1100 miles away, but it is beyond all reason in price and only for great occasions can one afford a head.

Military Display from British North American Fleet, 1894

CHAPTER NINE

September 1895 – March 1896

"The gun sounds – the mail closes"

Since St. John's was dependent for its communications on the erratic comings and goings of the mail ships which were governed by such variables as tide, weather and cargo, it was the custom for the gun on Signal Hill to be sounded when a mail ship was about to leave as a warning to all concerned to rush their mail to the departing vessel before it raised anchor. So Brother Slattery had ended his letter to the Superior in June with: "The gun sounds — the mail closes." Now the gun was sounding for Brother Slattery himself. What had happened to his letter of resignation of the previous year? His resignation was really unnecessary; normally a Brother was appointed in charge of an establishment for a term of six years. He had already served his six years and could expect to be replaced. So the school year began with Brother Slattery waiting for word regarding his future.

After six turbulent years, his final year was surprisingly tranquil. In September the CHE exam results were published and St. Bon's had done well again. John Fenelon obtained the top prize; three out of the five scholarships were secured by the College, including one by young Brother Anthony Murphy; and twenty-three of the thirty-five available prizes were won by the College students. In the Junior Grade, James Benning got second place and Ronald Kennedy, George Kearney and James Pippy won prizes. No one from the College passed the London Matriculation Exam, but Brother

Benedict Sullivan was awarded first division in the Intermediate Arts examination of London University, the highest exam ever attempted on the Island.

Because of the economic problems subsequent to the bank crash, there were fewer boarders to start the year with, but the number gradually increased. The new Bishop of St. George's, Bishop Neil McNeil, visited the College in November and was much impressed by what he saw, reporting to Bishop Cameron, his counterpart in Antigonish that "his [*Bishop Cameron's*] College is way behind St. Bonaventure's."

In December, Brother Andrew Prendergast became ill of a strange nervous disorder. Although he recovered within a short time, this was the first warning of a disease which would become increasingly severe as time went on, cut short his teaching career and plague him for the remainder of his life until his death in New York in 1954.

Brother Slattery also was not well and was looking forward to his release from office. In January 1896 came the news which he had been awaiting. The Superior General wrote on January 8:

> As your term of Office has expired and that you have expressed the wish to be relieved from the burthen, I am about to accede to your request. You will then as soon as convenient make up your accounts and arrange outstanding debts in connection with the College. And then when you have all done kindly let me know, say, by telegramme. I will then give further directions.

Considering all that Brother Slattery had gone through and the remarkable success that had crowned his efforts, one would have expected at least some acknowledgement of what he had done and some expression of gratitude on the part of the Superior, but this, sadly, is lacking in the Superior's communication. Brother Slattery must have been hurt by its absence.

In early March Brother Slattery wrote back, suggesting that he leave at the end of the month when the financial quarter would be complete. On March 24, a telegram arrived recalling him to Ireland to become part of the Brothers' community in Waterpark College, Waterford. Brother Joseph Crehan was appointed to succeed him.

When the news of Brother Slattery's departure became known, there was an outpouring of affection and regret. *The Evening Telegram* stated: "Universal will be the regret that a gentleman of such masterly executive ability and extensive learning is so soon to sever his connection with the educational institutions of this colony." Two days later, Brother Slattery, hearing that a testimonial was about to be taken up, wrote the editor of the *Telegram* in terms that were somewhat theatrical perhaps, but revealing of his character:

Dear Sir:-

I see by the morning *News* that some good friends of mine are taking action regarding a souvenir or presentation of some kind to me. I am profoundly grateful for this other link to the long chain of kindness I have received from the people of St. John's for the past fifteen years. But, considering the state of financial matters generally, the many bitter wants of our poor people, and the thousand claims on the restricted funds of all, I must positively decline the acceptance of anything involving the outlay of money. I own and can own no property. My wants are few and simple, and they have been fully, nay, *abundantly* satisfied during my residence in St. John's. In this matter I am sure my kind friends will fully appreciate my motives and do me the favour of complying with my wishes.

My time is so occupied now and so very limited, I fear I may not be able to say good-bye to many dear friends on whom it would be a sad pleasure to call. I avail myself of this opportunity to ask their kind indulgence and to accept this informal farewell. Wherever my life's pathway may lead me, I shall never forget the dear friends I leave behind in Newfoundland.

Testimonials began to pour in, but Brother Slattery must have cherished especially that from Mr. W. W. Blackall, Principal of Bishop Feild College, in which he said that Brother Slattery was leaving behind "many friends of all Creeds, and, as far as I know, no enemies." He noted that Brother Slattery and himself, though differing in religion, had "pulled the same stroke" in educational matters and he trusted that his successor "may have the breadth of sympathy and generous heart of my friend."

Brother Slattery's last full day (March 30) in Newfoundland was a hectic one. Because of his premature departure, the Annual Distribution of Prizes was brought forward to that morning. Following the usual awarding of prizes, Harry Strapp and John Fenelon, on behalf of the boys, presented Brother Slattery with an address and a silver watch. During the day, pupils from the Mercy Convent came to the College to present him with an address and "a beautiful bronze crucifix and font."

That evening, Brother Slattery was present at St. Patrick's Hall for one of the regular lectures he had arranged for the winter season. The Hon. George H. Emerson was the speaker, his topic "A Tour Through Europe." When St. Bonaventure was mentioned and Brother Slattery referred to, the audience broke out into spontaneous applause. Brother Slattery was forced to come forward while the boys of the Irish Society, under Professor Hutton, sang "Auld Lang Syne." Brother Slattery attempted to reply but "memories of other days had flashed to his big broad mind and he could not trust himself to say more than 'thank you' and to call for three cheers for Newfoundland."

Although space has precluded extended mention of it in this story, Brother Slattery had been a strong advocate of the physical development of the boys, and on his return to the College from St. Patrick's Hall, the Shamrock Cricket Club came at 9:30 p.m. to present an address to one who "had been its honorary vice-president and principal benefactor."

The next day, the day of his departure, *The Evening Telegram* saluted him with a long description of his career in Newfoundland topped by his picture—an unusual event in the papers of the time. Then there appeared in the *Evening Herald*'s MARINE MATTERS the following brief announcement: "The *S. S. Grand Lake*, Captain Delaney, sails for Halifax at 4 p.m. She has small freight and following passengers: Rev. Bro. Slattery..." What a depth of emotion there must have been in the breast of Brother Luke Slattery as he left behind, presumably forever, the land he had learned to love so well and had served so faithfully.

CHAPTER TEN

Epilogue

*B*rother Slattery's later career can be briefly told. In assigning him to Waterpark College, it had been hoped he would get a well-deserved rest, but events frustrated this plan. His successor, Brother Joseph Crehan, broke down almost immediately after being appointed President and had to be recalled to Ireland. In this emergency Brother Bernard Lavelle, the senior teacher at Waterpark College, was rushed to St. John's in early September and Brother Slattery was asked to take over his duties in Waterford.

This situation lasted only a year, however, for in September 1897, Bishop Howley wrote to Brother Maxwell saying that he had received a formal commitment from the Newfoundland government to support children at the proposed Catholic orphanage at a rate roughly equivalent to the cost of maintaining such a child in the penitentiary. He therefore urged Brother Maxwell to send Brother Slattery back to Newfoundland immediately to start this orphanage so as to copper-fasten this agreement "while the iron is hot" and so secure the grant from "any effects of fluctuating politics." Bishop Howley was only too well aware of the contradictory attitudes of the various political parties in Newfoundland.

And so Brother Slattery returned to St. John's in October 1897 after only eighteen months absence to be welcomed by the Bishop and the people with open arms. Unfortunately, between the receipt of the letter of agreement from the Colonial Secretary and the enactment of legislation to enshrine it, a new government came into power and repudiated the agreement. Because of the compelling need, and trusting in Divine Providence, The Bishop and Brother Slattery decided to go ahead anyway, the Bishop donating his own family property for the purpose. In spite of immense difficulties, within ten years Brother Slattery had succeeded in establishing the orphanage on firm grounds.

The cost to him, however, was high. Brother Slattery had squandered whatever emotional and physical energies that still remained in him. In 1907, in failing health, he was recalled to Ireland again and retired to the North Monastery, the Brothers' celebrated school in Cork, where he remained until his death three years later at the age of sixty-three. He is buried in the monastery cemetery next to another famed Christian Brother, the novelist and poet Gerald Griffin. It is interesting to note that in the same monastery a young Brother was experimenting with the development of an "underwater boat." Some years later he left the Brothers, moved to the United States and invented the first successful submarine. Holland Tunnel in New York is named in his honour.

And what about the novitiate? When Brother Lavelle arrived in St. John's, he found he could not cope with all the demands upon him, and he had the novitiate closed. The novices were transferred to Ireland to continue their training. Some of them, naturally, did not persevere, but those who did gave noble service to the Congregation. After completing his training, Brother Benedict Sullivan was transferred to South Africa where he spent most of his life at Christian Brothers College in Kimberley until he was recalled to Ireland, and then to England where he died in 1943 at the age of sixty-six. Brother Vincent Strapp and Brother Cyprian Walsh spent their entire lives at St. Bon's except, in Brother Strapp's case, for a three-year interlude as Superior of Mount Cashel Orphanage. Brother Cyprian died at St. Bon's in 1943 at the age of eighty, and Brother Vincent died there in 1952 aged eighty-five. Brother Dominic McCarthy was to have a long and distinguished career in the Congregation, obtaining his PhD at a time when such degrees were a great rarity and serving several times as principal of various high schools in the United States. He died in New York in 1968 aged 87. One has to admit that the monastic regimen did not injure the longevity of any of these men.

While the novitiate was closed after such a short time, while it was in operation it showed that Newfoundland boys had the character and spirituality to persevere in the religious life. Perhaps this is why, when the newly formed North American province of the Christian Brothers opened its first novitiate in 1916, all three of the first group to enter were Newfoundlanders: Brothers Patrick Keane, Ignatius Murphy, and Joseph Donnelly. All three persevered to a ripe old age in the Congregation, Brother Keane being the last to die in 1996 at the age of ninety-six.

How are we to sum up the achievements of Brother Slattery? He took over a run-down institution on the verge of collapse and in a few years built it into the leading educational establishment in Newfoundland. Between boys and staff he inspired a unique spirit of mutual respect, trust, self-confidence and friendliness which was the wonder and envy of similar educational establishments in the island. St. Bon's gave students, whether in academics, school sports or adult life, the ability to face challenges with confidence and perseverance This spirit endured throughout the entire life of the College and enabled its ex-pupils to reach the highest levels in civil or ecclesiastical life.

Brother Slattery also established the first organized teacher-training program in the colony. He was the guiding light in the reform of the educational system of the island, a reform which raised the system to a much higher level, and which endured for a hundred years to the great benefit of the Island. His enterprise in entering students for the London Matriculation Exams made the authorities of the other denominations realize that Newfoundland students were far more capable than they had believed, and the other Colleges quickly caught up with St. Bon's in this enterprise. His advocacy of teachers helped raise teaching to a true profession with proportionate financial reward. His warm relations with the other Colleges established a pattern which persisted, in friendly rivalry, until the eventual demise of all three. The greatness of his vision, his courage in the face of adversity, his humility under rebuke, his sympathy with the poor, all these qualities made him a man whom the *Evening Herald* described as one "with a heart large enough to embrace the world."

Did he have faults? He would not be human if he did not, but these were faults which arose from his strengths. The depths of his compassion for the poor of Newfoundland meant that he was continually devising new means of helping them without counting the cost to himself. His reach continually exceeded his grasp. The reverse side of this coin was that he could not give to his religious duties all the attention that they deserved and which was necessary if he was to maintain his spiritual strength. It was because of this problem that he lost from the community Brother Flood and his valuable cultural services; it was why he was in fairly constant difficulty with his Superiors in Ireland. It was probably because of this that the noble experiment of the Newfoundland novitiate was terminated with the result that no other Newfoundlanders joined the Brothers for the next twenty years, a lack which severely restricted the educational apostolate of the Brothers in both Newfoundland and Canada for many years.

Still, such weaknesses are an inevitable part of our human nature. In Brother Luke Slattery, they were greatly overshadowed by his accomplishments and the benefits he brought to his adopted country. At the time of Brother Slattery's departure from Newfoundland, the well-known Newfoundland poet, Dan Carroll, marked the occasion in verse. Included on page 87, it expresses well the sentiments of the people for Brother Luke Slattery.

Like tear-dimmed eyes when friends depart,
Our city lights looked out to sea,
Our city, whose deep, grateful heart
Low-sobbed a sad good-bye to thee:
And many a friend upon the quay,
That midnight when you sailed away,
Who watched thy ship the Narrows passed
Till gleamed one beacon from her mast,
Heard through the mist the distant roar
Of billows telling to the shore
In language all could understand:
"A MAN is leaving Newfoundland."

Appendix 1:

OFFICIAL REPORT, 1890
OF THE SUPERINTENDENT OF EDUCATION,
J. J. WICKHAM, ESQ.

The total income was $4,659.48, made up of the annual Legislative grant of $3,465.48 and receipts from fees $1,184. The expenditure, owing to the outbreak of diphtheria among the resident students in December 1889, was unusually large, amounting to $5,734.07. Of this the sum of $970.50 was expended in the purchase of new apparatus for the experimental study of physics together with a collection of mineralogical specimens, anatomical models and a varied assortment of objects intended to illustrate the different processes used in the manufactures. A considerable outlay was also incurred and laying out and improving the College grounds.

Despite the alarm occasioned by the outbreak of diphtheria in the College, the attendance for the past school year was larger than for any year since 1886. The whole number of pupils enrolled was one hundred and sixteen, of whom forty-one, including twelve pupil teachers, were resident students.

The accommodations provided for these students comprise every arrangement calculated to ensure their health and comfort, the appointments of the dormitories, refectories, recreation-rooms, gymnasium &, being all that could be desired. While all possible pains are taken to promote the physical well-being of the students, as well as their intellectual development, no effort is spared to cultivate in them a high standard of manly conduct and to form their character upon sound moral and religious principles. The inner government of the institution is directed with great care; and the discipline throughout, while thoroughly effective, is equally removed from that undue stringency and espionage which generally breed distrust and antagonism and that mistaken laxity so conducive to the growth of careless or vicious habits...

With respect to the scholastic work of the past year, which I had the opportunity of testing just before the Christmas vacation by a careful examination extending over four days, it affords me pleasure to be able to speak in terms of unqualified satisfaction. The admirable organization of the schools, the excellent discipline maintained and the well-directed enthusiasm of the teachers were reflected in the orderly behavior of the pupils and the eager interest which they displayed in their work. The students were grouped in five classes. The work of the fifth class [lowest] embraced a knowledge of English grammar as far as syntax, elementary parsing, analysis and composition, reading and spelling in fourth book, the compound rules and simple proportion in arithmetic, the outlines of geography with particular reference to the British Isles and Newfoundland, the outlines of Newfoundland history and elementary drawing.

The fourth class was doing more advanced work in the same branches, with the fifth reader instead of the fourth, and had begun the study of French. Several of the pupils in this class were particularly quick and intelligent in their answering.

The third class read with careful enunciation in sixth book, had a good knowledge of etymology and syntax, as set forth in the Christian Brothers class-book, together with the analysis of simple sentences and more advanced exercises in composition. In arithmetic, considerable facility was shown in vulgar fractions and interest. The work of this class in French was a stage more advanced than that of the last-mentioned, comprising about eighty exercises of Ahn's first book. At this stage the study of book-keeping, by single entry, and elementary algebra was introduced and the history of Newfoundland gave place to that of England. This class, on the whole, were well up to the mark in all the branches and bore themselves with creditable self-possession.

The second class, numbering twenty pupils, read with pleasing expression in sixth book, had attained a more advanced knowledge of grammar and analysis, with more ambitious efforts in composition and a more minute acquaintance with the geography of Great Britain and America and the history of England. In arithmetic, the class had mastered vulgar and decimal fractions and the different rules involving the principle of percentage, such as Profit and Loss, Stocks, &c. The work in algebra had been extended to embrace a knowledge of all the simple rules from an elementary text-book and, in book-keeping, to double entry. The study of French, from Ahn's first book was continued, about one hundred exercises having been gone over. While their pronunciation would not perhaps come quite up to the Parisian standard, they were thoroughly familiar with the grammatical construction of sentences, as far as they had gone, and showed considerable facility in the correct rendering of easy English sentences into French and *vice-versa*. In this division, the study of Latin was taken up, pupils being well-grounded on the first part of Smith's Principia, to the end of Passive Voice; and natural philosophy was also introduced. I was pleased to observe in the work of this class, as a whole, an evidence of talent and power of sustained application which promise well for their future success.

The students of the first class, six in number, under the special care of Rev. Brother Crane [sic]... were following the programme of the London University matriculation examination for June 1891.... I trust some of the members of this class will be encouraged to present themselves at the examination for matriculation in the London University to be held in June next, when the Newfoundland Jubilee Scholarship (value $480 per annum for two years) will be open to competition.

I was pleased to note that drawing was taught to all the classes in the College; and that the study of vocal music according to the Tonic Sol-Fa system was pursued with much zest under the direction of Rev. Brother Flood. St. Bonaventure's was thus the first educational institution in the country to introduce this new and popular system.

It had been arranged to hold the customary public exhibition of the College at the usual time, just before the

91

midsummer vacation; but the Principal having been summoned to Ireland early in June to represent this colony in the decennial convention of the order held last summer in Dublin, it was found impossible to carry out this arrangement. At the close of the Christmas term, however, the postponed exercises were carried out with much success in the presence of His Lordship, Dr. Power, and other members of the Board of Directors and the clergy of the city and outports; and valuable prizes were distributed by His Lordship to the most successful students.

The success of the first year's work of the College under the new regime holds out a most encouraging prospect for the future of academic education in the denomination and fully vindicates the wisdom of the Board of Directors in placing the active management of the institution under the control of the Christian Brothers. Without disparagement to the many clever and accomplished gentlemen, lay and clerical, who guided its destinies in times gone by, it must be admitted that the present faculty enjoy opportunities for successful work which were impossible under a different system of management. Members of a body specially devoted as teachers to the practical work of education, they have no outside matters to distract their attention and can concentrate all their energies upon the work which is their main object in life—their only earthly ambition being a desire to attain greater skill and realize higher ideals as instructors of the young. The peculiar organization of the Society, too, affords a powerful stimulus to constant effort in this direction, all members before their final reception into the Order, being subjected to a progressive series of yearly examinations, intended to test both teaching ability and scholarship, extending over several years. The success which has attended the operation of their schools in Ireland, in India, in Australia and other parts of the British Empire bear ample testimony to the effectiveness of such a policy for the development of thoroughly competent teachers.

It is, I consider, a matter for congratulation to the Catholic people of the country that the management of our chief seat of learning is in such competent hands. In the Principal, Mr. Slattery, the institution possesses an enlightened and progressive head, a gentleman of great experience in the work of education, a skilful disciplinarian and a capable administrator; while he has the good fortune to be aided by a staff of teachers whose devotion and skill are visible in the results of their work. I have every confidence that under its present management, the institution will maintain a leading position among the educational establishments of the Colony and continue to place within reach of our youth the means of acquiring a liberal education upon the solid basis of morality and religion.

Appendix No. 2:

Essay on Improvement of Education in Newfoundland
Bonavista (Br. J. L. Slattery)

I. System

With machinery more or less perfect, there is a system of Education established in the Colony which, on the whole has done good work. If the results are not satisfactory, the cause may be found in the apathy of the people, and in the circumstances of the Island. With all its defects it may be claimed for this system that it has not caused any ill feeling among the members of the different religious denominations, and that no charge of proselytism under its wings has been made.

Many persons advocate the abolition of the denominational principles on which it is based. They forget the cost of the risk. Each religious body has made great and praiseworthy efforts, and has expended vast sums of money in furtherance of its particular views regarding Education. Without noticing the work of former times, witness the splendid new college raised by the Methodists, St. Patrick's Hall and the schools in Riverhead by Catholics; and the fine building erected near the Synod Hall by the members of the Church of England. Looking through the Island, the educational establishments not erected on the denominational principle, are conspicuous by their absence. Uproot this principle and private efforts are at an end. This is the one green spot in the great desert of dependence on government for supplying every want, public and private, I regret to say it, but the fact cannot be denied, that the people look to each successive Government, more and more, for those things they should procure for themselves.

Any material change in this matter will disarrange the present machinery, create distrust, and perhaps stir up religious discord. If we look to some of the neighbouring provinces, notably Manitoba and Ontario, not to mention the

United States and some countries of the Old World, the frightful risk will be seen of having an educational system out of harmony with the feelings of a considerable section of the population.

The main object of this paper is to show how the present denominational system may be retained, yet so improved so to give results satisfactory to the people and to the Government. Beyond voting the annual subsidy, no Government in recent years has done anything to foster education, or to encourage a spirit of study among the youth of the Island. If efforts similar to those advocated below were made by those in authority a new state of things would soon be manifest.

THE CHANGES ADVOCATED ARE:-

(a)   The improvement of the teachers' position by increase of salary, by rewards for satisfactory results etc.
(b)   More efficient inspection by a proper distribution of the work, and by the establishment of an Educational Bureau.
(c)   Fostering a spirit of emulation among pupils, teachers and School Boards.
(d)   Providing for certain districts, not able to support schools for each denomination.

Details on each of these points will be found later on.

II. Inspectors etc.

(a)   One Inspector could never do the work of examination throughout the Island, much less attend to the clerical duties connected with office work. Three at least are required, and even with that number a proper distribution of the work must be made, so as to have it done efficiently. I need only mention the issuing of three Reports as a specimen of the useless loss of time and money the Colony is now enduring.
(b)   The Colony could be very conveniently divided into three districts: - One, including the settlements in the neighbourhood of St. John's and extending from Harbour Grace to Burin. Another from Harbour Grace North. A third from Burin Westward.

St. John's should be excluded from these districts, as each Superintendent could easily examine the schools of his denomination at any convenient time.

Each inspector could take a district in rotation, In this way the work could be efficiently done, and no denomination run the risk of unfair treatment*

(c)   A Central Council of Education representing proportionally each denomination, could be much in the interests of Education. But on no account should it be connected with the Government. Should it be so connected, politics would glide in imperceptibly and party spirit rule in a matter that should be above party and the heat of politics. The members of this Department might be named by the heads of the different denominations and approved by the Governor in Council.

The status and duties of this Board are suggested later on.

(d)   I fail to see any necessity for an Educational Depot in St. John's. It would interfere with the vested interests of those engaged in the trade, and could not do much that the different stores are not doing now. The expense of such a Depot would not allow prices to be much lower than at present.

III. Taxation

No per capita taxation could be raised in this Colony at present. The people have been trained to look to the Government for everything, that a great prejudice would be created against any Educational system resting on the basis of direct taxation. I daresay a sufficient revenue for all Educational purposes could be raised by an Income Tax, thus benefitting the poor at the expense of those who are able to afford the means. I see no other source of taxation. If the government liberally seconded local efforts much could be done to train the people to do something for themselves. For instance, in the erection of schools, if the Government gave a dollar in addition to each dollar raised locally, great efforts would be made to supply local wants. I fear, however, that, for the present, the public funds must be the source from which all Educational wants are to be supplied.

IV. Compulsory Attendance

(a)   The whole question of compulsory attendance is a complex and difficult one. Many of the best friends of Education hold very divergent views on the matter. Doubtless some compulsory is necessary, but the circumstances of the island would make it both difficult and impracticable. Something might be done in large centres, but in sparsely populated out-harbours, where it is most necessary, very little could be effected by its means. Any form of compulsion will create ill-feeling towards the system and a dislike for Education in general. Far better to foster a love for the schoolroom and a desire for improvement. If prizes were open to the best pupils in a district, if clever and promising students were helped on, there would be no necessity for compulsion. One pupil winning a prize of $10.00, would do more to fill the forms of the village school than would all the compulsion the Government would bring to bear. At the same time if the local policeman had orders to get a list of attendances from the teacher, and to summon the parents of the absentees before the nearest Magistrate, something might be done; but great liberty of action should be left in the hands of the Magistrate.
(b)   If it were thought well to establish any law of compulsion it should affect children from six to fourteen years of age. The distance of the school and the age of the child should be taken into account. Children of six or seven years should not be bound to attend unless the school were within half a mile of their home. Children of eight, to attend if within one mile; those from nine to fourteen years, if within three miles. No child should be bound to attend if the school were beyond three miles.
(c)   Making allowance for bad weather, distance, etc., a minimum of six attendances (½ days) per week should be exacted.
(d)   There is a long distance between enacting and exacting penalties for such matters, and it is just here that the imprac-

ticability of compulsion, in this Colony, shows itself. Fine or imprisonment might be the prescribed penalty, but inability to receive Government aid in any form would be a strong inducement with the class likely to offend.

V. Teachers

(a)   Three grades of teachers seem to be the simplest arrangement and as this system of classification is already in existence, no change need be made. Preserving the local machinery now existing, I would allow the School Boards the disposal of funds as at present, while the teachers' salaries could be supplemented according to grade. The Central Education Board alone should grant grade certificates on the recommendation of the three Inspectors, and each teacher taking out such certificate should.reeeive his grade salary direct from this Board, on the affirmation of the Chairman of any local Board that such teachers had charge of a school in his district. In this way the position of the graded teachers could be improved without disturbing the present local arrangements.

(b)   I should suggest that in addition to their present salaries, teachers should be paid according to the following scale:-

	1st Grade	2nd Grade	3rd Grade
Males	$100	$50	$25
Females	80	40	20

Teachers' salaries should be increased also according to the state of their schools. On the report of the Inspector as to whether a school were 3rd, 2nd, or 1st Class a bonus of $50, $30, or $10 should be allocated. If reported as unsatisfactory no bonus should be given by the Central Boards.

(c)   If the position of the teacher be improved, as suggested in the previous and following paragraphs, there should be no necessity for any Life Assurance.

(d)   Every effort should be made to retain experienced and graded teachers in the service. The Colony has expended some $300 on the training of each, and they have acquired that experience which is indispensable in a good teacher. Yet the present system almost drives them away just when they are of most use to the Education of the Colony. After five years teaching the salaries should be increased $40, $25, and $15, according to grade. A similar increase should take place after ten years service and the maximum salary reached by a third increase after fifteen years teaching.

No further increase need be made, and the teacher might retire after thirty years service. He would then cease receiving a salary from the Local Board, but should enjoy his full class salary as a pension. If a teacher, after completing fifteen years service, were obliged to retire from ill-health, etc., he might receive one-thirtieth of his grade salary for every year served. No teacher retiring before fifteen years service to receive any pension. Every teacher should be compelled to retire at sixty years of age. According to this scheme, a teacher would have three sources of revenue:-

(a)   His salary from the Local Board.

(b)   His salary according to grade, with the increment from long service.

(c)   The bonus arising from the Report of the Inspector.

To show the working I will take a few typical cases.

A first class teacher would continue to receive his present salary of (say) $250 from the Local Board. The Central Board would pay him $100 as his grade salary. If the Inspector reported very favourably of his school he would receive a bonus of $40. In all he would receive nearly $400 per annum for the first five years. For the second period of five years $440; for the third period $480; and after fifteen years he would have over $500 per annum. After thirty years service he might retire on a pension of about $250 per annum.

A second class teacher receiving (say) $160 would receive his grade salary of $50 and a bonus of $30 or $40, that is about $240 per annum for five years, $265 for second period; $290 for third and $315 as maximum; retiring on $150 (about) after thirty years service.

A teacher of third class receiving at present $120 would get the additional grade salary of $25, with such bonus as the

Inspector adjudged, (say) $30; in all $185, increasing after five years to $200, etc. He would retire on about $110 per annum.

To some persons this might appear a very low salary, but when we remember the exceedingly meagre attainments necessary (at present) in a third class teacher, I cannot see how the Colony can afford more.

Others might look on the proposed scale for first as too high. Every encouragement should be held out to teachers to attain the highest point of their profession and none whatever given them to remain in the lowest grade.

Ungraded teachers to get no salary from Central Board.

VI. Exhibitions and Scholarships

The present Jubilee Exhibition should be abolished, as it has has no effect on the Education of the Island. Its place should be taken by other smaller and more easily obtained exhibitions tenable for two years at any of the Academies or Boarding schools of the Island. I would suggest that five such exhibitions, of $150, per annum, should be open every year, This would give ten continually, and would cost $1,500, irrespective of clerical works.

The position of normal student should also .be won by open competition , and the best material selected on which the Colony is to expend its money.

Some of the unsuccessful competitors could get prizes of (say) $20, $20, or $6. I believe such competitors wold have a magical effect on the youth, the schools and the Boards of the Island. Without going into minute details, the plan might be a follows:-

(a) Pupils desirous of competing to make formal application to the Central Board before lst. April each year.

(b) Such applicants to undergo a preliminary test examination in presence of the Local Chairman and other members of the School Board, Sealed Examination Papers to be sent by the Central Board to all such Chairmen, so that the test examination could be held on the same date throughout the Colony.

The Chairman should be responsible for the proper conducting of the Examinations.

(c)   All the answers being returned to the Central office, the three Inspectors, having examined them, should certify to the Central Board as to the eligibility of the different candidates.

(d)   Those candidates found eligible might have their expenses to St. John's paid, according to distance. (The Kensington Department does this for certain students under certain circumstances.)

The object of the preliminary Examination is to hinder a number of unsuitable candidates coming up to St. John's.

(e)   Finally, the three Inspectors should prepare papers, assign marks, conduct the examination, and report to the Central Board.

Five having the highest marks to receive the $150 exhibitions at any College or Academy in the Island.

Of the other competitors a certain number might receive prizes as mentioned above.

(f)   The examination could be used to select candidates for the different Normal Colleges. The five exhibitions would be open to all denominations, but a certain number from each could be selected for free places in the Normal College. Thirty Normal teachers might be selected annually for a course of two years training. That would mean sixty in continual residence at $150 each. This would cost $9,000 against the $6,000 at present allocated.

The thirty could be distributed according to proportion of population, (say) eight Wesleyans, ten Episcopalians, and twelve Catholics.

Competitors for Exhibitions should be under fifteen years on the first of April in the year in which they are examined. Those competing for free places in the Normal Colleges should be under sixteen years.

In these competitions students should be assigned numbers by which only they should be known to the examiners. In this way there would be fair play all round.

The subjects for examinations should be:- English, including Spelling, Dictation, Parsing, Grammar, Geography, History, Composition, Mathematics, Arithmetic, Geometry, Book-keeping and Algebra.

VII. Mixed Schools

(a)   If in a district, any one denomination can muster an average attendance of twenty children, they might have a School Board and School of their own.

(b)   If other bodies united can muster twenty in average attendance, they might have a separate Board representative of the different bodies.

(c)   If no one denomination can muster an average of twenty children a common school should be established and a Board, composed of representatives of each denomination, could be nominated.

(d)   In no school receiving aid from Government should any religion instructions be given to a child except with the parents knowledge and consent.

(e)   Funds for supporting these mixed schools should be allocated by the Central Board from the grants to each denomination.

VIII. Central Board

A central Board should be established, its members being representative of the different religious denominations, Its functions should be:-

(a)   To issue the Annual Report.

(b)   To provide rules for the examination and grading of teachers, and to fix the standard of such examinations.

(c)   To frame rules and programmes for the examinations of candidates for Exhibitions, Prizes, and free places at the different Normal Colleges.

(d)   To issue certificates to teachers, and pay their salaries, with the increments advocated above.

(e)   To sustain the opening of new schools, and superintend the disposal of funds allocated to the different school boards.

In conclusion, I would claim for the system herein outlined that it preserves as much of the present plan as has been found useful, encroaches on no religions principle, can give offence or irritation to no denomination, raises the status of the teachers as much as the circumstances of the Colony allow, and will give a new life and a new spirit to all persons connected with Education—to pupils, to teachers, and to School Boards.

I am etc.
"Bonavista"

Rev, Br. J. L. Slattery

Appendix No. 3:   ST. BONAVENTURE'S
                                        January 9, 1895

Editor Daily News

Dear Sir,

It is rather dangerous for any one to venture to express an opinion on the present crisis. Party feeling runs so high, people are so intensely interested, they are so aggrieved, that calm discussion of this most grave question is almost impossible. Yet I think it is a duty each one owes to the colony, to cast any light he may be able on the gloomy situation. Having no policy to defend, no party to attack, no patronage to gain, I feel some confidence that my remarks will be taken in a good spirit as they are dictated only by a love for the colony and for the welfare of its people. I repeat no party is attacked or defended in what follows.

I have diligently read what has appeared on all sides of the question, and in the House of Assembly, have listened with interest, pleasure and admiration to the able advocates of the different policies. Should any one who does me the honor to read what follows, not agree with the reasons alleged or the conclusions deduced, I shall be happy to be set right, and have the weak links in the chain pointed out. By the destruction of its weaker points, my position will be the more strengthened.

As a remedy for the present crisis, three proposals are before the public:—

(a) The government should guarantee the full face value of the notes of both banks.

(b) The government should guarantee not only the noteholders but the depositors also.

(c) The recent act of the Legislature guaranteeing 80 cents and 20 cents on the respective notes.

It is only natural that all noteholders should advocate the first, and that depositors should call for the second of these proposals. As both are agreed in asking the colony to stand by the banks, I shall discuss the proposals together.

To guarantee the face value of these notes, either there is gold behind them or there is not. If the colony can borrow at once two million dollars, the notes can get their face value, not otherwise. A pawn ticket, a mortgage bond, or a bank note derives all its value from the fact that it represents material goods, that is, gold. A bank note in itself costs about a cent. If gold is behind it, it is worth its face value, if there is not, then it is worth nothing.

From the fact that no one advocates this enormous loan to back their proposals, I gather that the notes are not to have gold behind them. This is proved further by a proposition to have them redeemed in a number of years. In other words no specie can be got for these notes till the expiration of the proposed time. The instant it is felt that there is no gold behind these notes, immediate depreciation will be the result. The value of the paper will fluctuate according to the probable assets of the bank, and the proximity of specie payment. The effect of issuing inconvertible paper money or of suspending specie payment for money in circulation is changing the standard of value, and is a debasement to the coinage, no matter what the wording or act of Parliament may be.

When a country issues paper money not payable on demand, the value of the currency slips away from all fixed reckoning. The first relief from the difficulty is so pleasing as naturally to lead to a larger and larger issue, and the delusion is prolonged till the situation begins to be disclosed. Gradually specie passes out of the country, foreign exchanges become more and more difficult, the notes begin to lose their usual purchasing power, provisions and all goods advance in price, and the day begins to dawn for the heartless money lenders.

How can this depreciation be measured? A convertible paper currency maintains its par with gold by being payable on demand in the gold it promises to pay. So the depreciating note falls as much below par of gold, as the difference between the amount of gold it *professes to be*, and the amount of gold it exchanges for its (money?) market. In technical language the price of bullion increases along with the price of other commodities.

In this matter the Legislature is powerless, and fifty Acts of Parliament cannot make a bank note worth more than the amount of specie behind it. The amount procurable for a bank note will always be the real value of that note, no matter what any Act of the Legislature may say to the contrary. No more certain lesson is taught by the history of finance all the world over. I shall mention only a few cases.

Just one hundred years ago the leaders of the French Revolution seized on the Church lands and ordered them to be sold. From many causes no purchasers could be found, no sales could be effected. At last corporations were allowed to purchase them for notes called *assignats*. These were to be payable in specie, when the lands were resold to private individuals. With these notes the Government paid its debts, and "the *assignats* saved the Revolution;" but, having no specie behind them, they gradually depreciated till they were worth only one hundredth of their face value.

Owing to the wars of Napoleon, the Bank of England suspended specie payments in 1797. The value of its notes steadily depreciated each year till it reached its lowest point in 1813 when the £5 note was worth only seventy-three shillings (73s.) Then an increase gradually set in till 1821, when specie payments were resumed.

In 1866 Italy issued a forced paper currency of Treasury notes. Depreciation at once set in, and in 1874 gold was at a premium of thirteen.

A worse state of matters still exists in some of the Republics of South America. In Argentina the currency consists wholly of paper notes, ranging from one cent up to $100. In 1884, when specie payments were suspended, the dollar was worth ninety-six cents, but at the close of 1890 it was worth only thirty-seven cents.

If the notes of the Bank of England, of France and of the United States were worth only a fraction of their face value when specie was not behind them, what possibility is there that notes, similarly circumstanced in this colony, will not at once become depreciated? Let us examine some of the consequences.

1st—When depreciated money circulates in the country, the direct result is always to have real money disappear. Each person trying to get rid of the *uncertain note,* and to retain the certain coin, gold is gradually withdrawn from circulation, and from the country. Hence the proverb, *Bad money drives out good money.*

Again, all foreign exchanges are based on the fact that there is gold behind somewhere. Much of the foreign exchange, no doubt, is done by exchange of goods, yet the amount of gold transferred is very great, and depends on the balance of trade between different countries. I owe $100 in London, and I have $100 in notes. What am I to do? I cannot send the notes to London; they would be useless there, and I can get a bill of exchange in London only at a discount corresponding to the depreciation of the notes.

Whatever may be the inducements to enter on the perilous course of tampering with the standard of money, universal experience has proved its disastrous effects.

But, it is said, "Make the notes a legal tender, and then every one *within the colony* must take them." I can understand the "man in the street" speaking like this, but it is a mystery to me how any thoughtful person can express such an idea. If the notes were legal tender at face value, the Government should receive them in the Customs House, and consequently should pay its current expenses with them. The salaries of officials, the grant for the poor, the various calls for civil administration, the dividends to debenture holders should be paid in these notes. But the interest to foreign bond holders should be paid in gold. *So dividends to our own people would be paid in depreciated paper, but those to foreigners should be paid in solid gold.*

But then "the trader should take them for face value in payment for goods of all kinds." The immediate result would be a rise in prices all round, the notes losing their usual purchasing power. While the notes would be of face value, the increased prices would express the amount of the depreciation. This would be about the same as if the notes had lost part of their face value.

At present a pair of boots costs five dollars. If the dollar note depreciates to 50 cents, I must pay two five dollar bills for the boots. *This is the depreciation of the face value of the notes.* But the Legislature says the note must not be depreciated, must be taken at its face value. The price of the boots must at once be advanced to ten dollars. *Now the depreciation is seen in the increase of price,* though the face value is nominally retained. So it comes to the same thing in the end, whether the notes are made legal tender or not.

Even a greater evil would follow from this arrangement. We should have in the colony two kinds of money: one, these legal notes, which every one should take for their face value; the other, gold and notes (American, etc.) not depreciated. The prices of goods and provisions would be regulated by the value of the depreciated notes. For a good American five dollar bill or for an honest English sovereign, I could get no more goods here than for our own depreciated five dollar note. What would follow? I should send my sovereign to England and my five dollar bill to the States, where I could get, perhaps, twice the value for each of them. This again proves the axiom that "Bad money drives away good money."

From what has been said, these conclusions inevitably follow:—

1.   A forced paper currency will be certainly a depreciated one.

2.   The amount of depreciation will depend on the proximity or remoteness of payment in specie.

3.   If Union and Commercial notes are guaranteed at face value in a certain number of years, depreciation will set in, and this will be the discount off the face value.

4.   If made legal tender at face value, the depreciation would be shown, by an increase in the price of goods. In other words, the notes would lose their present purchasing power.

5.   The real depreciation would be the same in both cases.

I fear I have trespassed too far on your space, and so shall come to an end for the present.

Very truly yours,
J. L. Slattery

Brother Strapp with his primary class, 1899

Senior Class, c.1899

Sport's Day, 1890s

School Play

Hockey on campus, 1890s

Catholic Cadet Corps, 1890s

Cricket Champions, 1901, Captain J. Pippy (future Father Pippy)

Intercollegiate champion team, football sixes, 1902

Council of Higher Education, c.1920

Bishop Howley, Brothers and distinguished ex-pupils, c.1906

Joseph Bertrand Darcy was born in St. John's, Newfoundland, and received his entire elementary education at St. Bonaventure's College. It was the custom at St. Bon's that each student should have the broadest possible education; therefore, although young Darcy achieved the highest scholastic level possible, graduating first in his class, he was also a member of the orchestra (violin and piano) and a member of both the basketball and football (soccer) Intercollegiate teams.

Upon graduation from St. Bon's, Darcy attended Fordham University where he received his B.Sc. Summa cum Laude (first in class), Education M.A. — philosophy. His studies in music led to receiving his ATCL from Trinity College of Music.

In October 1936 James Darcy joined the Christian Brothers in New York.

Brother Darcy's teaching career was broad and varied. He taught at Iona Preparatory School, St. Bonaventure's College, Rice High School (New Your), lectured at Iona College in New Rochelle, N.Y., and at the Christian Brothers Intermediate School in Belfast, N. Ireland.

Brother Darcy has also held a number of administrative posts including Dean of Scholastics, Iona College; President, St. Bonaventure's college; President, Newfoundland Teachers Association; Board of Directors of Canadian Teachers Federation; Assistant to Provincial, American Province of Christian Brothers; First Provincial of Canadian Province of Christian Brothers; Vicar General of Christian Brothers (Rome).

In retirement Brother Darcy continues to be an active member of the community serving as a member of the Museum Committee, Basilica of St. John the Baptist; writing a monthly historical column in the archdiocesan newspaper, the *Monitor*; hosting a weekly broadcast, *Reflections of Faith*, on Radio Station VOWR and is currently researching and writing a book on the life of one of Newfoundland's most influential church leaders, Bishop Fleming.